BY ADAM STARCHILD

*The Seafood Heritage Cookbook*

*The Amazing Banana Cookbook*

(with James Holahan)
*Starchild & Holahan's Seafood Cookbook*

# The Seafood Heritage Cookbook

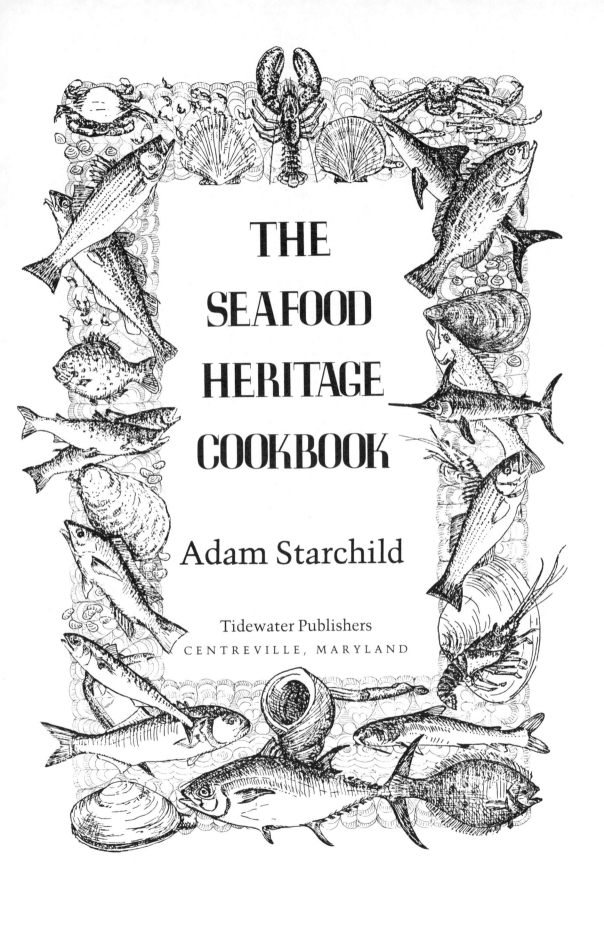

# THE
# SEAFOOD
# HERITAGE
# COOKBOOK

## Adam Starchild

Tidewater Publishers

CENTREVILLE, MARYLAND

Library of Congress Cataloging in Publication Data

Starchild, Adam.
The seafood heritage cookbook.

Includes index.
1. Cookery (Seafood)     I. Title.
TX747.S657   1984     641.6′9     83-40549
ISBN  0-87033-312-7

Manufactured in the United States of America

First Edition

# Contents

Introduction
3

How-To and Basic Techniques
7

Appetizers and Soups
19

Salads
39

Main Dishes—Fish
53

Main Dishes—Shellfish, Crabs, Squid, Etc.
109

Microwaving Seafood
141

Sauces, Marinades, Dips, Dressings, Stuffings, Etc.
149

Index
177

The Seafood Heritage Cookbook

# Introduction

The culinary habits of Americans are as diverse and varied as the many nationalities that have settled our country. Each nationality has brought its own preferences and idiosyncracies in the preparation of food. Because of a strong desire to recreate the environments left behind, these immigrants developed cooking methods and recipes with many regional and ethnic overtones. However, in spite of these differences, the use of seafood as a major and highly palatable source of protein has provided a culinary common denominator. Surprisingly, there is little recognition of the use of seafood as part of our ongoing national heritage. This heritage has taken shape slowly over the years as the varied methods of preparing seafood practiced by the inhabitants of North America have influenced each other to finally produce a unique agglomeration.

Since early American colonists shared a common understanding of the value of food from the sea, they made commerical fishing one of their chief industries, an industry that persists in importance to this day. Perhaps there is no better way of emphasizing the significance of seafood to the colonists than to quote Benjamin Franklin's letter to Sir Francis Bernard:

> I have no receipts for pickling either sturgeon or salmon, but will endeavor to procure you one for sturgeon. In my opinion a great deal depends on the kind of salt to be used. For this I would refer you to Brownrigg's book where you may find what salt the Dutch use for their herrings. There is an alkaline corrosive quality in common course salt, which must be corrected by some acid in the boiling and refining of it. The Dutch use buttermilk, I think, for that purpose.

Seafood was first harvested in abundance along the American coastline. As the pioneers began pushing inland they left the sea behind, but found the interior of the continent abounding with lakes and rivers which were teeming with fish. It was of little importance, it turned out, that these inland fish were different species from those left behind; for example, the good Swedish housewife who migrated westward with a husband bent on mining gold in the Rocky Mountains soon learned that trout taken from the cold sparkling waters of the mountains were as tasty pickled by traditional Swedish recipes as were the seagoing fish of her old country.

Of course, it wasn't long before American ingenuity found a way to supply inland dwellers with these delicacies from the sea; for example, it is reported that Mr. and Mrs. Abraham Lincoln hosted frequent oyster feasts in Springfield, Illinois. Later, but still long before the advent of highly sophisticated methods of preserving seafoods, regions far from the sea such as Colorado and central Kansas enjoyed perfectly fresh seafoods on traditional "fish days" (Fridays—of course).

As our seafood heritage has been perpetuated and strengthened, so have the myths and legends that have sprung up concerning the eating of seafood. Here are a few:

*Oysters and other shellfish should be eaten only in months with an "R" in them.* This is not true of shellfish harvested commercially in the United States.

*Oysters are an aphrodisiac.* By connotation an aphrodisiac is a drug used to create sexual desire. Although the oyster is one of nature's most wholesome foods, it certainly does not fall into this category.

*Shellfish that die before being cooked should not then be cooked and eaten.* This is not entirely true, as shellfish that die before being cooked do not become toxic. Shellfish do, however, quite quickly develop an off-flavor due to enzyme digestion of the flesh, and are not as palatable as shellfish cooked live.

*Seafood is a brainfood.* Unfortunately, this is currently supposed to be untrue. Science recognizes no food as "instant brain food"; however, studies have shown that the nutritional value of seafood is excellent, and, properly nourished brain cells do perform with increased capacity. Starving cells do not.

*Eating seafood with fresh milk will make you sick.* Not true, no combination of two wholesome foods can make you sick.

*Frozen seafood is inferior to fresh seafood.* If seafood is frozen by the best available methods, and is fresh when frozen, it is not an inferior product. As with any other kind of food, problems such as "freezer burn" can develop due to incorrect freezing methods. Fish held too long before freezing, or fish that have been frozen, thawed at room temperature, and refrozen, will almost surely develop off-flavors and odors. However, if you happen to be unlucky enough to buy this kind of product, don't blame seafood *per se*, blame the market or restaurant where you purchased it. It is axiomatic that in the fishing industry, more people have been turned away from seafood through fish held too long in ice or refrigeration than for any other reason.

The more science learns about nutrition, the more emphasis it places on eating seafood. For example, a serving of sole fillet contains over twenty times more protein than fat, as compared to approximately one and a half times more protein than fat in a serving of beef that is eighty-six percent lean, eleven percent fat, with bone. The added health bonus is that the fats of the fish contain a higher ratio of unsaturated to saturated oils. Furthermore, in order to take in the recommended daily allowance of protein, about twice the number of calories must be consumed in a serving of beef as in a serving of fish. These are important reasons for the consumption of fish. However, since most Americans will continue to eat what they like in spite of nutritional considerations, the most important argument for eating seafood is its amazing variety and delectability, and the number of different ways in which it can be prepared.

This latter feature is what this book is about. Whatever your national origin or ethnic background, you can venture within the pages of this book and quite possibly find an Americanized version of some seafood dish brought here by your forebears. But, be forewarned, readers of these recipes run the danger of becoming cosmopolitanized and equally addicted to Tuna and Noodles Italian Style as to Creole Jambalaya.

# How-To and Basic Techniques

One reason why many more Americans haven't developed a "taste" for seafood is because of the high perishability of all seafoods which, in less than ideal conditions, can mean a product that is still usable but off-flavored and strong smelling. Another important factor in fish flavor is the proper cooking method. Fresh seafood should never taste "fishy." It should taste sweet and mild when properly prepared. Fish should be a real delicacy to all but the very few, who, probably through some psychological aversion, really can't tolerate the looks or taste of any fish. In this chapter we will explore the whys and hows of properly handling and preparing fish.

The three obvious ways of obtaining fish are by purchasing it in a market or from a commercial fisherman; by catching it yourself; or by having it given to you by someone who must have obtained it by one of those methods.

By far, the best place to buy fish is in a market which has good access to the freshly caught product, and which does a large volume of business in fresh fish. If this isn't possible, you might do well to search out a market where you can talk to the fish buyer, who can tell you which day of the week the product arrives at the market, at which time it will be its freshest. The third alternative is, unfortunately, the gleaming supermarket where most fresh seafood is packaged in cellophane, a product which effectively conceals (though not deliberately) any off-odors that might have developed through too-slow handling. Of course, the frozen-breaded products, such as fish sticks are always available in the frozen food case, but these are only a good buy if you prefer convenience foods.

If you are fortunate in having a market to shop from, which features fresh fish, please note the four ways in which the fish are prepared for market, which are: round, cleaned and headed, steaked, and filleted.

Fish in the round are those which haven't been eviscerated or headed. This is not a popular consumer product, and is therefore offered in only a few markets, primarily those that specialize in fish and have a few target customers for this product.

A cleaned and headed fish is one that is destined to be baked whole or in a large chunk, cut into steaks or fillets by the consumer, or pan fried. Salmon are frequently sold this way.

Generally, any fish sold without being cut up will still have the skin on it, and, depending on the species, may also have scales. The scales should be removed, but the skin is usually left intact during cooking, to be removed before eating.

Steaks are cut from certain species of fish by first eviscerating the fish, then slicing crosswise across the body to obtain steaks, which will still contain the skeletal bones of the fish. Steaks usually range from one and one-half to two inches in thickness. This is a popular way of marketing salmon.

Fillets are slabs of boneless or near-boneless meat removed from the bony skeleton of the fish. Most bottom fish, such as flounder, sole, etc., are marketed in this manner. The more expertly a fish is filleted, the thicker and larger the fillet will be for a given species. Commercially filleted fish will also have the skin removed by the time they arrive at market. A fish is usually filleted without being eviscerated, as eviscerating would just be an unnecessary step. Filleting is more a science than an art, requiring a sharp knife and the experience to do it quickly and well. Fillets are an excellent buy for the budget conscious, since they are cut from the relatively inexpensive, though tasty and nutritious, species, and are virtually waste free.

When buying fresh fish from the market, note that the following are evident:

The eyes are clear, full, and bulging.

The gills are reddish pink and free from slime.

The scales adhere tightly to the skin and are bright-colored, with the characteristic sheen of the fish.

The flesh is firm and elastic, and springs back when pressed. A cut surface should have a waterlike shine.

There is no objectionable odor, in fact an iced or refrigerated fish only a few hours from the water should have no outstanding odor. For fillets, check the edges for odor; for whole fish, check the belly area.

Frozen fish are a good alternative to fresh fish, providing you are reasonably sure they were frozen properly and before being held too long. Some fresh fish markets offer specials on bags of frozen fillets which are classed as "miscuts" (a miscut is a fillet not up to certain standards of thickness, size, etc.), or which are in surplus of what the market could move quickly.

Considering the length of time that a fresh fish might have been held in ice or refrigeration, you should handle it quickly after the purchase and plan not to hold it longer than another 24 to 48 hours in your refrigerator. Plan a shopping trip so that the last items bought are the fish, and don't leave fish in a warm car for even as long as two or three hours. Fish that aren't cooked the same day they're purchased should be wrapped in moistureproof paper and stored in the coldest part of the refrigerator.

If you are within weekend driving distance of the coast, or public ponds, or sportfishing regions, you may catch your own fish, or alternatively, buy a few months' supply of freshly caught fish at the source of catching (be sure, however, that your fish merchant can legally sell you the fish, in order that you don't become involved in an unlawful transaction). Ocean fish such as bottom fish should be filleted as soon as possible, preferably at the site. Most coastal areas have public cleaning stalls and/or professional filleters who will provide filleting for a fee. Shoreside filleting will save a lot of ice and storage space on the return trip, as well as the problem of refuse disposal at home. A salmon should be eviscerated and scaled (but not skinned), and if it's too large to fit into the ice chest whole, it should be cut into pieces appropriate to the planned cooking methods. If you do the work yourself, wash the cleaned fish or fillets in running water before packing them in the ice chest; then, using a generous amount of ice to surround the fish, pack them in the ice chest, and get them to refrigeration as quickly as possible.

An ice chest full of filleted fish will create a surplus over normal family use and should be frozen. Rule number one is that the quicker you get your recently caught and iced fish into the freezer, the better they will taste two months later. The best way to package fillets or steaks for freezing is in the closeable plastic bags which are waterproof when closed. Measure out meal-sized portions into the bags, cover the fish with water, and seal the bag. Baking size chunks of whole fish should be frozen in moistureproof-vaporproof paper, and should probably be used ahead of the fish frozen in ice, as the latter will remain fresh tasting longer. Any pan-size fish, such as freshwater trout, can also be frozen in bags of water.

For best keeping qualities, the temperature of the freezer should be zero degrees or lower. Even at optimum temperature, raw frozen fish shouldn't be held longer than six months.

If fish *must* be kept for two or three days without ice, refrigeration or freezing, they can be preserved for this short period of time by salting. Here's how:

Cut the fish into fillets (see "filleting" later in this chapter), and cover all the surfaces with as much noniodized salt as will cling to them, using about one cup of salt for each five pounds of fish. Pack the fillets in a deep container for four to six hours, then remove them from the container and rinse off any excess salt. Wipe the pieces dry and keep them in a cool place.

## Cleaning Fish

Different species of fish require different cleaning methods; however, the tools of cleaning are essentially the same for most fish: a sharp knife, suitable for either filleting or eviscerating (usually available at a sporting goods store); a stone with which to keep the knife sharpened; and for filleting, pliers or grippers. All fish cleaning areas should have running water.

## Cleaning Trout

Freshwater trout don't have scales. Your trout should be eviscerated as soon as possible after being caught. Hold the fish belly-up in one hand, and with the other hand insert the point of the *sharp* knife in the vent. The knife should be pointed toward the head. Slit the trout open from the vent to the gills. When you reach the gills, cut them out in their entirety as nothing indictes a sloppy cleaning job more than remaining gill portions. Use your hand to remove entrails completely, noting that some of the stuff virtually falls out, while some must be worked loose from such areas as the rib cage and backbone. Everything must come out clean, and when the backbone is exposed, you will see a membrane-covered vein of blood running the length of the backbone. Use the point of the knife, or a fingernail, as a scraper to remove this vein. When the inside of the fish is completely clean of viscera and blood, wash it out with running water. Most people prefer to take home pan-size trout with the tail, skin, fins, and head still intact.

## Cleaning Catfish

Eviscerating a catfish is done about the same way as a trout, but please note, or soon unpleasantly find out, that the "feelers" on the catfish's head are needle-sharp and to be avoided. Catfish are generally headed and skinned before being cooked. However, some people prefer to fry small catfish with the skins on, peel them after cooking, or just before eating. Larger catfish are sometimes filleted.

## Cleaning Salmon

Except that its skin will be covered with scales, any species of salmon is just an oversized trout where cleaning is concerned. Logically, scaling should be the first step in the cleaning operation; to do this, lay the fish on its side, and holding the knife blade vertically with the blunt edge against the fish, scrape off the scales, working from the tail toward the head. Wash the fish thoroughly before continuing with further cleaning. After washing, eviscerate (see Cleaning Trout), and cut into pieces as desired. If your fish must be cut up to fit in the ice chest, make the initial cuts so that the larger, fleshier center cut can be used for steaking, and the smaller and/or bonier portions for baking.

If you receive a salmon that has been cleaned but not scaled, as might be the case if a friend gives you one, soak it in cold water for a few minutes before scaling. Avoid leaving any scales sticking to the flesh of the fish.

## Filleting Bottom Fish

Your first experience at filleting bottom fish won't be easy, but will be worthwhile when you realize that the washtub full of uncleaned fish will translate into a small ice chest only partly full of fillets. The cleanup factor for bottom fish is about thirty-three percent, or, about fifty pounds of whole fish will yield about fifteen to seventeen pounds of fillets.

Most bottom fish have tough skins and all have scales. Some people leave the skins on fillets, in which case the fish should first be scaled. However, the better method is to remove the skin during the filleting operation, making scaling unnecessary. Some bottom fish are flat (flounder, sole, etc.), while others have a body more like a trout or salmon. In either case, the goal of filleting is the same: to remove meat from the bony carcass in large slabs from each side of the fish, leaving the bony skeleton as clean of flesh as possible. To do this on the flat type of fish, lay the fish on either side, slit along the backbone as if separating the two halves of the fish, then, starting at the tail, with the knife blade held as nearly flat as possible, cut toward the head, slicing the slab of meat away from the bones. As you finish the cut you'll have to do some separating and cutting around the head area to remove the fillet. Turn the fish over, and repeat the procedure on the other side. Generally, a flat fish is fleshier on one side than the other. When both fillets are removed, the waste part of the fish will be the tail, carcass, head, and viscera, which must be discarded in such a manner as to not attract the neighborhood cats and dogs.

To remove the skin from the fillets, peel it away from the tail end far enough to be able to grasp it with the pliers or grippers, then, lay the fillet skinside down on the cutting board, and, with the knife blade almost flat, simultaneously pull on the skin and push and cut with the knife until the skin and flesh are separated. Ideally, there will be no flesh left clinging to the skin, nor any pieces of skin adhering to the fillet.

To fillet the full-body type of fish, such as lingcod, use a sharp knife to cut through the flesh along the back ridge from the tail to just behind the head. With the fish on its side, slice the flesh cross-wise just above the collarbone until the knife gets down to the backbone. With the knife's edge working at a flat angle toward the tail, cut the flesh from the backbone and rib bones. Lift off the entire side of the fish in one piece. Turn the fish over and fillet the other side.

## Thawing Frozen Fish

Frozen fish may be thawed in the refrigerator for 24 hours, or if quicker thawing is necessary, place the package under running cold water, allowing one to two hours for each pound of fish. Never thaw fish at room temperaure or in warm water. Frozen fillets or steaks can be cooked without prethawing, but you can do a better job of cooking if the fish is prethawed. To be breaded, steaks and fillets must first be thawed.

## Cooking Fish

The most common mistake of the inexperienced fish cook is *overcooking*; and then, in overcompensating on the second attempt, *undercooking*. When, during the cooking process, the watery juices of the raw fish become milk covered and the flesh takes on an opaque, whitish tint (in the case of a white-fleshed fish) to the center of the thickest part of the fish, it is completely cooked and should be removed from the heat. At this point the flesh should be easy to flake off the bone.

## Poaching Fish

To poach a fish, wrap it in cheesecloth and place it in a wire basket, being careful not to lay fillets or steaks on top of each other. Simmer gently in enough water to cover the fish. For each four cups of water add one-half teaspoon of salt and one tablespoon of vinegar or lemon juice. Add spices, herbs, and milk or wine to taste. Simmer until the fish flakes easily, usually from five to ten minutes.

## Steaming Fish

To steam a fish, wrap it as for poaching and place it on a rack above boiling water. Cover the pan tightly and steam for twelve to fifteen minutes per pound, or until the flesh flakes. Season the fish after removing it from the steamer.

## Steaming Fish—Oven Method

To steam a fish in the oven, wrap in aluminum foil, making sure that the wrap is airtight by double folding the top and pinching in the sides of the wrap. Place the wrapped fish on a shallow pan and bake at 450 degrees, allowing fifteen minutes cooking time for each unfrozen one inch thickness, or 25 minutes per inch of frozen fish. An albacore cooked in this manner can then be skinned, and the meat quite easily flaked from the carcass, ready to be used in your favorite recipe or equally ready to go into sterilized canning containers and be processed for future use.

## Baking Fish

Baking, with or without stuffing, is one of the more popular methods of cooking fish. Dry a dressed fish and sprinkle it lightly inside and out with salt and pepper, allowing one-half teaspoon of salt and one-eighth teaspoon of pepper per pound of fish. Rub the fish with oil or butter, or lay strips of bacon over it. Bake in a greased pan at 400 degrees for ten minutes per pound of stuffed fish. When done, the fish should be nicely browned, and the skin will be loose enough to peel off quite easily.

## Broiling Fish

Broiling is the preferred method of cooking fish for many dieters since this method adds minimal calories. Brush the fish with butter or lay pieces of bacon over it (or use no oil if your diet so dictates), and place it two to six inches from the broiler, which has been preset at 375 to 400 degrees. Broil until well browned, then turn and broil on the other side. Add salt and pepper after the fish is turned. Fillets or steaks require five to eight minutes broiling on each side, depending upon their thickness. To broil a whole fish, season with salt on the inside and brush lightly with salt, pepper, and butter on the outside. Broil about ten minutes on each side.

## Frying Fish

Any fish is almost always breaded or dipped in batter before frying. For best results, both the quality and cooking temperature of the oil should be closely controlled. Therefore, use a good vegetable oil and try to regulate the cooking temperature to about 350 degrees. The fish may be French fried, being sure that pieces do not overlap and touch each other in the fry basket. Generally, when the battered or breaded pieces are golden brown, the fish will be done. To fry fish in a pan, use enough oil to come *halfway* up the pieces. Maintaining the 350-degree cooking temperature (about MEDIUM on most electric ranges) put the battered or breaded pieces in the preheated oil, cook on one side until golden brown; then turn and cook on the other side until golden brown.

## Oven Frying Fish

Oven frying is not really frying, but a hot oven method that produces a taste similar to that of pan frying. Cut the fish into serving size portions, dip in salted milk, and coat with toasted, fine, dry bread crumbs. Place in a shallow, well-greased baking pan, pour a little melted butter or oil over the fish, and bake at 500 degrees. The fish does not require turning, basting, or close watching; the cooking time is usually about ten to fifteen minutes. This is an excellent way to cook fish.

## Smoked Fish

Smoked fish are a delicacy (and priced accordingly, you'll find, when you go to buy some).

Before smoking a fish, it should be brined; however, before starting either of these processes, you should buy or make a smoker. Many sporting goods stores offer smokers, or you can build your own. To make your own smoker from a fifty-gallon drum, cut out the top with a chisel or cutting torch (if the old barrel contained any volatile liquid such as gasoline, as a safety precaution fill the barrel completely with water before cutting out the top by any method). Reduce the diameter of the removed top by about three inches; suspend this top from three brackets, thirteen inches below the top of the open drum: This is the *heat baffle*. Next, cut an eight by ten inch section from the side of the drum, near the bottom: This is the *fire pit opening*. To cover this opening, make a door out of the lightweight sheet metal and attach it to the barrel with a single hinge. Next, out of one-quarter or one-half inch mesh, make a tray that will fit inside the barrel; suspend this tray inside and about six inches below the top of the barrel by hanging it from metal straps: This is the *smoking tray* which holds the fish. Now, to finish your barrel smoker, use a metal or wooden cover over the top of the barrel; This will be your *draft control*, as you move it around to enlarge or reduce the size of the top opening.

Steaks, fillets, or whole fish can be smoked. Wash the pieces thoroughly, and soak them in a brine consisting of one and one-half cups of salt to one gallon of cold water. Keep the fish in this brine for at least twelve hours at forty degrees Fahrenheit. Preferred containers for brine are as follows: earthenware crocks, unchipped enameled pots, glass containers, and last but certainly not least, a *new* plastic garbage can for large brining jobs. (Never use a garbage can for food matter unless it is new and has been thoroughly cleaned and sterilized.)

Remove the fish from the brine, drain and rinse them, then place them, skinside down, on the smoking tray. Insert a short stemmed meat thermometer in the thickest part of the largest fish or thickest steak or fillet. Also hang an air thermometer inside your smoker.

To build your smoking fire, start with wood and build up a good bed of coals (charcoal briquets can also be used to develop the initial bed of coals) in the bottom of the smoker. Add a few wood chips; then, to keep the fire smoldering without flaming, add wet wood chips every half hour, or as needed.

Oak, hickory, maple, alder, beech, apple, white birch, or ash wood chips and/or sawdust produce good smoke. Don't use any pitchy wood such as fir, spruce, or pine.

When the temperature inside the smoker reaches 100 degrees, place the smoking tray with the fish in the smoker, taking care that the pieces of fish do not touch each other, and that the pieces are about the same size. Then, cover the smoker, keep the coals smoldering, and check the thermometers once in a while. When the air temperature is about 225 degrees inside the smoker and the fish temperature about 180 degrees, maintain these temperatures for about thirty minutes to cook the fish; this cooking inhibits bacterial action. Total smoking time is about four hours.

As soon as smoking is complete, wrap the fish in waxed paper and place in the refrigerator. Fish stored at temperatures not over forty to forty-five degrees should be used within a month.

## Pickling Fish

Pickled fish are a delicacy, as well as a viable way to use up a surplus catch of fish. The best pickled fish I have ever tasted were processed in the same brine mixture as that used for crisp, sweet pickles, by a precooking method that leaves the fish with a firm texture. Select the smallest fish, from the pan-size variety, for pickling. Use distilled white vinegar of no less than five percent acidity, noniodized salt, regular drinking water in ratio of one part water to one part vinegar, and the best quality spices.

## Selecting and Preparing Shellfish

Any shellfish, such as oysters, clams, crabs, etc., should be held alive until the moment they can be cooked. The traditional method of cooking most shellfish is to boil or steam them in the shell.

To prepare butter or littleneck clams by steaming, first scrub them under running water, then place them in a bucket of clean water, add one-half cup of salt and let them stand for a few hours while they clean themselves of sand. Next, place them in one inch of boiling water in a steamer or large kettle. Cover tightly and steam for ten minutes, or until the shells partially open. Detach the top shells, if desired, and serve the clams hot with side dishes of melted butter and cups of strained clam liquor.

To cook live crabs, plunge them *live* into salted and seasoned boiling water. Cover the pot to hasten cooking. Let the water return to a boil, and cook the crabs for about twenty minutes or until they turn red. To avoid overcooking, remove the crabs from the boiling water and place them under running cold water. The meat inside the crab shell is now cooked and edible, but must be removed from the shell.

There is more than one way to convince a crab to part with its meat, but some of these methods can be just plain frustrating. I believe this to be the easiest way to obtain lumps of meat rather than shredded crabmeat. First, begin by removing the claws by pulling them away from the body. Save any meat attached to the end of the arm. Then, holding a knife, similar to a boning or filleting knife, near the handle, use the knife as a club, of sorts. With the crab's claws against the tabletop, crack the claws and remove the meat in large lumps if possible.

Remove the shell that covers the back of the crab by grasping it near one of the spines and pulling upward. There will be no meat inside the shell, so you may discard it. In the middle of the crab will be a yellowish material, called fat, which you can scrape away with the knife. Some people like the fat, but most find it too strong. Cut away the gills, which are the feathery structures found on either side of the crab's back. Discard these; *they should not be eaten.* Next, cut away the walking legs; remove any bits of meat clinging to the cut ends; then crack the legs and remove the meat.

Cut the body cavity down the middle, then cut each half into several parts. With the point of the knife, remove the lump meat from the rear portion of the body. Now, remove the meat from the remaining sections of the shell by prying upward with the knife.

The crabmeat can be used for salads or in any of several recipes found in this book. Crab is high in protein and contains all the micronutrients necessary for good health.

# Appetizers and Soups

## Crawfish Canapé "Jacob Astor"

15 live crawfish
6 slices French bread
1 lemon
1 bundle fresh dill
⅓ pound butter
1 tablespoon curry powder

4 hard-boiled eggs
1 tomato (firm) 2½ inches in
    diameter
1 tablespoon plain gelatin
Salt and white pepper

To cook crawfish, bring a pot of lightly salted water (enough to cover the crawfish completely) to a boil. Add a head of fresh dill and lemon wedge (¼ lemon). Boil for a minute. Drop live crawfish into boiling water and cook at a slow boil for 5 minutes. Remove from stove and leave crawfish in stock for another 5 minutes. Remove crawfish and refrigerate until cold. Save stock for later use.

Next, toast French bread lightly. Soften butter and stir in curry powder to taste, and juice from lemon wedge. Press out bread with a wine glass or a round cookie cutter (approximately 2½ inches in diameter). Butter canapé generously with curried butter. Top with thin slice of tomato. Cross-slice hard-boiled egg in ¼-inch slices, remove yolk and top tomato with ring of egg white. With the hard-boiled egg yolks, make your favorite deviled egg filling. With a pastry bag using a star tube, fill in cavity in egg slice with a rosette of deviled egg filling.

Remove tail meat from crawfish. Save heads and claws for later use. Remove veins from crawfish tails and split tails lengthwise. (Split just 12 of the tails and leave 3 whole.) Arrange meat around egg rosette. Top with whole tail pieces and a piece of fresh green dill. Glaze entire canapé with light crawfish aspic.

To prepare crawfish aspic, strain 1½ cups of settled crawfish stock through cloth. Heat, add melted gelatin, strain again, and let cool. When mixture begins to gel, glaze canapé with light cover of aspic.

Arrange crawfish canapés on your favorite platter. Decorate with fresh dill, crawfish heads, and claws. Finish with lemon wedges.

Makes 6 canapés.

# Shrimp Paste Charleston

*With their knack for creating tasty and original dishes, Southerners have contributed much to American cuisine. Shrimp paste has been traditionally served for breakfast throughout much of the coastal South, although it is a particular favorite of Charleston.*

2 cans (4½ or 5 ounces each)
    shrimp or ½ pound cooked,
    peeled, and deveined shrimp,
    fresh or frozen
½ cup margarine or butter
2 tablespoons pale dry sherry

1 tablespoon lemon juice
1 tablespoon grated onion
¼ teaspoon ground mace
¼ teaspoon dry mustard
¼ teaspoon cayenne pepper
Assorted crackers

Drain canned shrimp. Cover canned shrimp with ice water and let stand 5 minutes; drain. Thaw shrimp if frozen. Put shrimp through finest blade of food grinder or chop as fine as possible. Cream margarine. Blend in sherry, lemon juice, onion, mace, mustard, and cayenne. Add shrimp, beat until smooth. Note that Shrimp Paste Charleston may be molded by placing paste in simple mold or container and refrigerating until firm. To unmold, loosen edge with thin-bladed knife, dip bottom in hot water, invert over serving plate, and shake gently until unmolded. Serve with assorted crackers.

Makes 1¾ cups.

# Shrimp Toast

1 can (4½ ounces) shrimp
2 eggs
1 tablespoon cornstarch
1 teaspoon sugar

2 teaspoons dry sherry, optional
⅓ cup finely chopped celery
6 slices bread, slightly stale

Drain and chop shrimp. Beat eggs well, with a wire whisk. Combine with cornstarch, sugar, and wine. Blend well. Add celery and shrimp. Spread mixture on bread, pressing and smoothing with the back of a spoon until it clings. Fill deep fry pan with salad oil to a depth of 2 inches or enough to float slices and brown without turning. Heat oil to 375 degrees F. or until it will brown a bread cube almost instantly.

Fry slices one at a time about 15 seconds, shrimp side down. Drain on absorbent paper. Cut in triangles.

Makes 12 or 24 hot appetizers.

## Seafood Cocktail

2 cups cooked shrimp, crab, or
    flaked fish
½ cup catsup
1 teaspoon Worcestershire sauce
2 tablespoons lemon juice

1 teaspoon onion juice
2 to 3 drops liquid hot pepper
    sauce
Dash salt

Chill fish and reserve. Combine all other ingredients and mix till well blended. Arrange the chilled seafood in cocktail glasses and serve with the sauce over the top. Garnish if desired.

Makes 6 servings.

## Pickled Herring—Norwegian Style

*Eating herring on New Year's Day is a tradition that was also brought to this country by many immigrants, and is still observed by many people to this day. The eating of the herring was believed to bring good luck in the coming year.*

8 medium-sized herring
¼ cup salt
1 quart water
1 sliced onion
¼ sliced lemon
2 bay leaves

1 teaspoon peppercorns
¼ teaspoon allspice
1 pint vinegar
1 pint water
Few whole cloves

Clean the herring, cover with 1 quart brine (¼ cup salt to 1 quart water) for 30 minutes. Remove fish from the brine and wipe dry. Place in a crock, alternate layers of herring and a mixture of onion, lemon, and spices. Cover with vinegar and water. Set the crock in a kettle of cold water. Bring water to a boil and let the mixture cook until meat drops from the bones. The herring is ready to use when cold. Keep in a cool place.

Makes 6 servings.

# Pickled Salmon

3 to 4 pounds salmon, in one piece
1 quart cooking water
2 quarts vinegar
1½ teaspoons nutmeg

6 blades of mace
1 tablespoon salad oil
1 ounce peppercorns

Wrap salmon in cheesecloth and simmer in salted water (1½ table-spoons salt to each quart of water) for 45 minutes, or until heated through. Drain and chill. Combine cooking water, vinegar, and spices, cover and cook 5 minutes; cool. Add salad oil to the cooled liquid and pour this mixture over the salmon; cover and store in a cool place. This pickled salmon will keep for several months.

Makes 6 servings.

# Kodiak Crab Sandwiches

*As early as the 1780s crabs off the Alaskan coast were an appreciated source of food. They were welcomed by seafarers whose diets consisted mostly of salt provisions. It wasn't until after World War II though that the Alaskan king crab fishery started to expand into a major industry.*

1 package (6 ounces) snow crab or other crabmeat, fresh or frozen, or 1 can (6½ ounces) crabmeat
1 cup shredded cheese
½ cup chopped celery
¼ cup chopped parsley
1 tablespoon lemon juice

½ cup mayonnaise or salad dressing
1 teaspoon Dijon-style mustard
⅛ teaspoon liquid hot pepper sauce
4 English muffins
¼ cup margarine or butter
8 sandwich-cut cheese slices

Thaw frozen crabmeat or drain if using canned crabmeat. Remove any remaining shell or cartilage. Combine crabmeat, shredded cheese, celery, and parsley. Combine lemon juice, mayonnaise, mustard, and liquid hot pepper sauce. Toss crabmeat mixture with this dressing. Split and toast English muffins; spead muffins with margarine. Place approximately ¼ cup of crab mixture on each muffin half and top with one slice of cheese. Broil about 4 inches from source of heat for 4 to 5 minutes or until cheese is melted and crab mixture is heated. To serve as an appetizer, cut each muffin half into quarters.

Makes 32 appetizers or 8 sandwiches.

## Golden Brown Sardine Appetizers

3 cans (3¾ or 4 ounces each)
    sardines
1 bouillon cube
⅔ cup boiling water
1 cup dry bread crumbs
¼ cup mayonnaise or salad
    dressing

1 egg, beaten
¼ cup finely chopped onion
2 tablespoons chopped parsley
1 tablespoon prepared mustard
½ teaspoon poultry seasoning
¾ cup cereal crumbs

Drain sardines and flake. Dissolve bouillon cube in boiling water. Combine all ingredients except cereal crumbs. Shape into small balls and roll in crumbs. Place on a well-greased cookie sheet, 15 × 12 inches. Bake in a very hot oven, 450 degrees F., for 10 to 12 minutes or until golden brown.

Makes approximately 45 appetizers.

## Alaskan Appetizer Pie

*By the late nineteenth century the Japanese had built a sizable king crab industry in the North Pacific. The American king crab fishery did not really begin in Alaska until the 1930s. Today the industry is flourishing with the harvesting of both king and snow crabs.*

1 can (6½ ounces) king crab meat
    or other crabmeat
1 package (8 ounces) cream cheese,
    softened

1 cup chili sauce
½ cup chopped parsley
Melba toast

Drain crabmeat; flake. Remove any remaining pieces of shell and cartilage. Spread cream cheese evenly in the bottom of a 9-inch glass pie plate. Cover with chili sauce. Top with the crabmeat and sprinkle the parsley over the crabmeat. Chill. Serve with melba toast.

Makes 3 cups.

## Plain Delicious Smoked Fish

5 pounds mullet butterfly fillets,
    fresh or frozen, or 3 pounds
    Spanish mackerel fillets,
    fresh or frozen

1 gallon water
1 cup salt
1 pound hickory chips
2 quarts water

Thaw fish if frozen. Combine 1 gallon water and 1 cup of salt. Stir until salt is dissolved. Place fish in brine and let marinate in refrigerator for 30 minutes. Remove fish from brine; rinse thoroughly and dry. Soak the hickory chips in 2 quarts of water for several hours or overnight. Keep chips in a cool place to keep them from taking on a mildewy or sour aroma. To smoke the fish, use a hooded or covered charcoal, electric, or gas grill. The heat must be kept low. If using charcoal, fewer briquets are necessary than for regular grilling. Cover charcoal or ceramic briquets with approximately ⅓ of the wet chips. The wet chips provide lower temperatures and create smoke which flavors the fish. Remaining chips are added as needed throughout the cooking process. Place the butterfly fish or fish fillets, skin-side down, on a well-greased grill, approximately 4 to 6 inches from the smoking chips. Close hood on grill and open the vent slightly to keep the smoke and air circulating. Smoke the fish approximately 1 hour at 150 to 175 degrees F., or for 30 to 45 minutes at 200 degrees F. Baste fish with cooking oil near the end of the cooking time. The fish is done when the cut surface is golden brown and when the flesh flakes easily when tested with a fork. This smoked fish can be used immediately.

*Note:* If fish fillets thicker than approximately ½-inch are used, the cooking time will need to be increased. Test for doneness near the end of the cooking time. If lean fish is used, baste frequently with cooking oil to prevent fish from drying out.

    The smoked fish can be held in the refrigerator at 35 to 40 degrees F., loosely wrapped, for 3 days with no loss of quality. To freeze, wrap the fish loosely and allow to cool in the refrigerator. Then rewrap in moistureproof-vaporproof wrapping, and place in the freezer. Smoked fish can be held up to 3 months in the freezer. To use, remove freezer paper, wrap in aluminum foil, and heat for 20 to 30 minutes at 300 degrees F.

Makes 6 entree servings and may be
used with a wide variety of dips.

## Calamary Mediterranée with Caper Sauce

2 pounds whole squid, fresh or
    frozen
2 tablespoons butter
2 tablespoons all-purpose flour
1 chicken bouillon cube
1½ cups water

¼ teaspoon salt
¼ teaspoon sugar
Dash white pepper
Dash black pepper
½ tablespoon capers
1 egg yolk, beaten

Thaw frozen squid. Clean squid if necessary. Cook mantles in boiling, salted water 1 hour or until tender; drain. Cut mantles into rings. In saucepan melt butter and stir in flour. Dilute bouillon cube in water and gradually pour into flour mixture. Add salt, sugar, white and black pepper, and capers. Stir in egg yolk and combine sauce with squid rings. May be served hot or cold as an appetizer.

Makes 12 servings.

## Country Crab Soup

1 pound blue crab meat, fresh or
    pasteurized
⅓ cup finely chopped onion
¼ cup finely chopped celery
¼ cup finely chopped green pepper
1 clove garlic, minced
1 tablespoon margarine or butter
1 can (13¾ ounces) condensed
    chicken broth, undiluted

1 can (12 ounces) tomato juice
1 teaspoon basil
1 teaspoon salt
¼ teaspoon thyme
¼ teaspoon pepper
3 to 4 drops liquid hot pepper
    sauce
1 package (10 ounces) frozen
    mixed vegetables

Remove any pieces of shell or cartilage from crabmeat. In a 3-quart saucepan, cook onion, celery, green pepper, and garlic in margarine until tender but not brown. Add broth, tomato juice, basil, salt, thyme, pepper and liquid hot pepper sauce. Bring to a boil. Reduce heat and simmer for 10 minutes. Add the mixed vegetables and simmer for another 10 minutes. Add crabmeat and continue cooking until vegetables are tender and the crabmeat is heated.

Makes 6 servings.

# Crawfish Bisque

*Crawfish bisque is to Louisiana what clam chowder is to New England. A thick soup containing cooked, ground crawfish meat, shells stuffed with spiced crawfish meat, chopped vegetables, and seasonings, it is a favorite of Louisianians. The state harvests more than 20 million pounds of crawfish each year, consuming up to 80 percent of this catch within its borders in the making of bisque and a wide variety of other dishes.*

## *Crawfish Preparation*

| | |
|---|---|
| 8 pounds live crawfish | 1½ cups salt |

Wash live crawfish in cold water. In a large container dissolve salt in about 3 gallons water and soak the crawfish for 15 minutes to purge. In a 10-quart pot bring 6 quarts of water to a boil. With tongs drop in the live crawfish and boil for 5 minutes. Remove crawfish and cool. Shell crawfish as follows: Break off tail, snap it in half lengthwise, lift out meat in one piece and discard the tail shell. Snap off large claws (if desired, break claws with nutcracker and remove bits of meat) and smaller legs; discard. Cut off top of head just behind the eyes; discard. Scoop the body shell clean. Carefully remove and reserve the yellow fat or "butter." Discard all intestinal matter. Clean and wash thoroughly 48 body shells, which in Louisiana are referred to as the crawfish "heads." Finely chop all the tail meat or put it through the finest blade of a food grinder. There should be about 3 cups of ground crawfish tail meat, 48 "heads" for stuffing, and the reserved crawfish fat.

## *Bisque*

| | |
|---|---|
| 1 cup ground crawfish tail meat | 2 cups finely chopped onion |
| Reserved crawfish fat | 1 cup finely chopped celery |
| ¼ cup bacon fat | ½ cup finely chopped green pepper |
| ¼ cup margarine or butter | 1 clove garlic, minced |
| ½ cup all-purpose flour | 4 cups hot water |

¼ cup chopped parsley
2 cans (15 ounces each) tomato
    sauce with tomato bits
2 tablespoons lemon juice
1 teaspoon dried thyme leaves,
    crushed

2 bay leaves
1 teaspoon salt
¾ teaspoon cayenne pepper
8 whole allspice
48 stuffed crawfish "heads"
3 cups cooked rice

In a 4- to 6-quart Dutch oven, melt bacon fat and margarine. Blend in flour. Cook, stirring constantly, over medium low heat until brown in color, about 15 to 20 minutes. Add onion, celery, green pepper, and garlic. Cover and cook 5 minutes or until tender. Gradually stir in water. Add parsley, tomato sauce, lemon juice, thyme, bay leaves, salt, cayenne, and allspice. Stir in remainder of crawfish meat after stuffing "heads." Add the reserved fat and cover. Bring to a boil and simmer for 1 hour. If desired, at this point you can drop in the stuffed crawfish "heads" so they will simmer with the bisque—or you may cook the heads separately and serve with the bisque as follows: ladle bisque into individual soup plates over boiled rice and drop in 5 or 6 stuffed "heads."

## Stuffed Heads

½ cup margarine or butter
1 cup finely chopped onion
½ cup finely chopped celery
1 clove garlic, minced
¼ cup chopped parsley
1 teaspoon salt
¼ teaspoon cayenne pepper

2 cups ground crawfish tail meat
2 cups soft bread crumbs
48 empty crawfish shells—
    "heads"
½ cup all-purpose flour
Fat for deep frying

In a 10-inch fry pan, melt margarine. Add onion, celery, and garlic. Cover and cook 5 minutes or until tender. Stir in parsley, salt, cayenne, and crawfish meat. Combine with bread crumbs. Stuff mixture into empty shells. Roll in flour. Place in single layer in a fry basket. Fry in deep fat, 350 degrees F., for 3 minutes or until lightly brown. Drain on absorbent paper. Keep warm until ready to serve.

Makes 6 to 8 servings.

## Crawfish Soup

⅔ pound fish bones and scraps
1 tablespoon cumin
¼ cup oregano
2 cups white wine
1 can (32 ounces) diced tomatoes
2½ onions
1¼ green peppers
⅓ bunch celery
¼ garlic clove

1 tablespoon fennel seed
1 tablespoon celery seed
1 small bay leaf, crushed
1 tablespoon sage
1 tablespoon whole or powdered
   coriander
2 teaspoons cayenne pepper
15 live crawfish

Fill a kettle to within 2 inches of top with water to cook fish bones and scraps; cool overnight. Strain and then add sautéed vegetables and seasonings and simmer for 8 hours. Meanwhile, *prepare the seasoned mixture below in which to cook 15 crawfish.*

1 cup mixed spice or pickling spice
¼ cup salt
2 quarts water

1 bottle (5 ounces) Worcestershire
   sauce

Boil these ingredients for 1 hour. Drop in the live crawfish and boil for 10 minutes. Remove from heat and cool. Drain crawfish; remove the meat and add to the soup shortly before serving.

Makes 6 to 10 servings.

## Cream of Shrimp and Lettuce Soup

1 can (4½ ounces) shrimp
1 head iceberg lettuce (weighing
   about 1½ pounds)
1 medium onion, sliced
2 cups water
1 tablespoon butter

2 cups cooked vegetables or
   2 chicken bouillon cubes
¼ cup heavy cream or evaporated
   milk
1 teaspoon salt
¼ teaspoon white pepper

Have shrimp chilled in the can. Trim and core lettuce; cut in fourths; place in a soup kettle with onion and 2 cups water. Cover and cook rapidly 5 minutes or until lettuce is wilted. Strain, reserving cooking water. Add butter and the vegetables (or if you prefer, bouillon cubes to make a thin soup) to the water and set aside. The vegetables should be precooked to the desired texture before adding to the water. Puree lettuce and onion in a blender. To the pureed mixture, add seasoned cooking water, cream, salt, pepper, shrimp, and shrimp liquid. Heat to blend flavors before serving but do not boil. Note that by using vegetables one time and bouillon cubes the next time, you will have two distinctive soups instead of one from this recipe.

Makes 5 servings.

# New England Clam Chowder

*Clam soups and chowders can be traced back to the eighteenth century where references can be found in diaries and letters. These early American soups were often made with salt pork, crackers, milk, and vegetables.*

2 dozen shell clams or 2 cans (8
    ounces each) minced clams
1 cup water
¼ pound salt pork or bacon,
    minced
½ cup finely chopped onion
1½ cups clam liquor, plus water

5 cups diced potatoes
2 cups milk
8 saltine crackers
2 cups half and half
2 tablespoons margarine or butter
Chopped parsley

Wash clam shells thoroughly. Place clams in a large pot with 1 cup water. Bring to a boil and simmer for 5 to 8 minutes or until clams open. Remove clams from shell and mince. Strain liquid remaining in pot. (Or: if using canned clams, drain and reserve liquor adding, if necessary, enough water to make 1½ cups liquid.) Cook salt pork until browned and crisp. Remove salt pork from pan, reserving 2 tablespoons of the drippings. In a saucepan, add onion and cook until tender. Add the clam liquor and potatoes and bring to a boil. As soon as the mixture begins to boil, reduce heat to a simmer and cook until potatoes are tender. Pour milk over saltines and let stand until soft. Stir the milk with the softened saltines, half and half, reserved salt pork, and margarine into the chowder mixture. Heat until hot enough to serve but do not allow to boil. Garnish with chopped parsley.

Makes 6 servings.

## Creole Bouillabaisse

*Bouillabaisse is one of the more famous dishes of New Orleans. It is a stew containing fish fillets, shrimp, oysters, crabmeat, vegetables, dry white wine, and seasonings. So impressed was Thackeray with bouillabaisse on a visit to New Orleans in 1856 that he later mentioned the dish in his* Roundabout Papers.

1 pound red drum fillets or other fish fillets, fresh or frozen
1 pound sea trout fillets or other fish fillets, fresh or frozen
½ pound raw, peeled, deveined shrimp, fresh or frozen
1 pint oysters, fresh or frozen
1 can (6½ ounces) crabmeat, drained and cartilage removed
2 tablespoons margarine or butter
2 tablespoons olive oil
¼ cup all-purpose flour

1 cup chopped onion
½ cup chopped celery
1 clove garlic, minced
5 cups water
1 can (1 pound) tomatoes, un-drained, cut up
½ cup dry white wine
2 tablespoons chopped parsley
1 tablespoon lemon juice
1 bay leaf
½ teaspoon salt
¼ teaspoon saffron
¼ teaspoon cayenne pepper

Thaw fish and shellfish if frozen. Remove skin and bones from fish. Cut each fish into 6 or 8 portions. In a 4- to 5-quart Dutch oven, melt margarine. Add olive oil and blend in flour. Cook, stirring constantly, until light brown in color. Add onion, celery, and garlic. Cook, stirring constantly, until vegetables begin to brown. Gradually stir in water. Add tomatoes, wine, parsley, lemon juice, bay leaf, salt, saffron, cayenne pepper, and about ¼ of the fish. Bring to a boil and simmer for 20 minutes. Add remaining fish and cook 5 to 8 minutes longer. Add shrimp, oysters, and crabmeat. Cook another 3 to 5 minutes or until all the seafood is done.

Makes 6 to 10 servings.

## Scallop Rémoulade Appetizer

*Scallop Rémoulade Appetizer is one of the outstanding Creole recipes of New Orleans. A blend of scallops, onion, parsley, lettuce, Rémoulade Sauce, dry white wine, and seasonings, Scallop Rémoulade Appetizer is an excellent way to introduce the main dish.*

1½ pounds bay scallops or other
    scallops, fresh or frozen
1 cup water
½ cup dry white wine
2 slices onion
2 sprigs parsley

½ teaspoon salt
¼ teaspoon thyme
Shredded lettuce
Rémoulade Sauce, see below
Hard-cooked egg, optional

Thaw scallops if frozen. Remove any remaining pieces of shell. Rinse with cold water and drain. In saucepan combine water, wine, onion, parsley, salt, and thyme; bring to a boil. Place scallops in poaching liquid; cover and simmer 2 to 5 minutes or until tender. Drain scallops and chill. Arrange scallops on a bed of shredded lettuce in individual seafood shells or in cocktail glasses. Spoon about 3½ tablespoons Rémoulade Sauce on top of each serving. Garnish with chopped hard-cooked egg, if desired.

Makes 6 servings.

## Rémoulade Sauce

¼ cup tarragon vinegar
2 tablespoons prepared brown
    mustard
1 tablespoon catsup
1½ teaspoons paprika
½ teaspoon salt

¼ teaspoon cayenne pepper
½ cup salad oil
¼ cup chopped celery
¼ cup chopped green onion
1 tablespoon chopped parsley

In small bowl combine vinegar, mustard, catsup, paprika, salt, and cayenne. Slowly add salad oil, beating constantly. (May also be done in a blender.) Stir in celery, green onion, and parsley. Allow to stand 3 or 4 hours to blend flavors.

Makes 1¼ cups.

# Oysters Rockefeller

1 pint oysters, selects or counts,
   fresh or frozen
¼ cup margarine or butter
¼ cup chopped celery
¼ cup chopped green onion
2 tablespoons chopped parsley
1 package (10 ounces) frozen
   chopped spinach

1 tablespoon anisette
¼ teaspoon salt
Rock salt
18 baking shells
¼ cup dry bread crumbs
1 tablespoon melted margarine or
   butter

Thaw oysters if frozen. In small saucepan melt ¼ cup margarine.
Add celery, green onion, and parsley. Cover and cook 5 minutes or
until tender. Combine cooked vegetables with spinach in blender
container. Add anisette and salt. Chop vegetables in blender until
almost pureed, stopping once or twice to push vegetables into knife
blades. (Vegetables may be run through a food mill.) Make a layer of
rock salt in pie tins. Place small baking shells or ramekins on top.
(The rock salt is used mainly to hold shells upright; however, it also
helps to keep oysters hot to serve.) Place the oysters in the shells or
ramekins. Top each oyster with spinach mixture. Combine bread
crumbs and 1 tablespoon melted margarine; sprinkle over oysters.
Bake in a very hot oven, 450 degrees F., for 10 minutes. Serve
immediately in pie tins.

Makes 6 appetizers (3 oysters each).

# Shrimp Christmas Tree

2 pounds medium shrimp, fresh or
   frozen
1½ quarts water
⅓ cup salt

3 bunches curly endive
1 styrofoam cone, 1½ feet high
1 small box round toothpicks
Seafood Cocktail Sauce, see below

Thaw frozen shrimp. Place shrimp in boiling salted water. Cover and
simmer about 5 minutes or until shrimp are pink and tender. Drain.
Peel shrimp, leaving the tail section of the shell on. Remove sand
veins and wash. Chill. Separate and wash endive. Chill. Starting at

the base of the styrofoam cone and working up, cover the cone with overlapping leaves of endive. Fasten endive to the cone with tooth-pick halves. Cover fully with greens to resemble a Christmas tree. Attach shrimp to tree with the toothpicks. Provide Seafood Cocktail Sauce for the dunking.

Makes 8 servings.

## Shrimp Boil

5 pounds shrimp, fresh or frozen
1 gallon water
1 lemon, sliced
1 small onion, sliced

½ cup salt
½ cup seafood seasoning
1 clove garlic, sliced
Seafood Cocktail Sauce, see below

Thaw frozen shrimp. Pour water into a large kettle. Add seasonings. Cover and bring to the boiling point over hot coals. Add shrimp. Cover and simmer for 5 minutes. Drain and serve with Seafood Cocktail Sauce.

Makes 30 hors d'oeuvre servings (generous), or if used as a cold dish for a main course, this will serve 15.

## Seafood Cocktail Sauce

1½ cups catsup
1 tablespoon lemon juice
1 tablespoon Worcestershire sauce

2 tablespoons horseradish
1½ teaspoons sugar
Salt and pepper to taste

Combine all ingredients and chill.

Makes about 1½ cups.

## Steamed Clams in Wine Broth

*The clambake is usually thought to be a New England tradition, but the Indians of the West Coast were also familiar with this way of cooking. The techniques were much the same. First, rocks would be heated in fires. After the flames died down the rocks would be covered with leaves, and seafood would be put on the leaves. Water would then be added, and the seafood would be covered with more leaves. The following recipe is based on those early clambakes, with a twist though—the use of wine for steaming that was introduced to the West Coast by the French.*

3 pounds littleneck or razor clams in the shell
½ cup dry white wine

2 tablespoons margarine or butter
½ cup melted margarine or butter
1 lemon or lime, cut into wedges

Wash clam shells thoroughly with a brush under cold running water. Using a large pot with a rack or a steamer, place wine and 2 tablespoons margarine in bottom of pot. Place rack in pot. Arrange clams on the rack. Cover. Steam for 6 to 10 minutes or until clams open. Arrange clams in their shells in shallow soup bowls and pour steaming broth over clams. Serve with melted margarine and lemon wedges.

Makes 6 appetizer servings.

## Pickled Rock Shrimp

2 pounds cooked, peeled, and deveined rock shrimp or other shrimp, fresh or frozen
½ cup salad oil
½ cup lime juice
½ cup sliced onion
6 lemon slices

1 tablespoon capers with liquid
1 tablespoon chopped parsley
½ teaspoon salt
½ teaspoon dried dillweed
⅛ teaspoon liquid hot pepper sauce

Thaw shrimp if frozen. Combine remaining ingredients. Pour marinade over shrimp; toss lightly. Cover and chill several hours, stirring occasionally. Drain. Note that this may be served on salad greens as an appetizer.

Makes 12 to 15 appetizer servings or
60 to 70 hors d'oeuvres.

# Salads

## Antipasto Salad

1 can (3½ or 3¾ ounces) albacore
    or other solid pack tuna
Crisp salad greens
⅓ cup potato salad
3 or 4 cucumber slices
2 radishes
2 carrot sticks or curls

2 ripe olives
1 green onion
½ hard-cooked egg
1 teaspoon capers
2 tablespoons mayonnaise
Lemon wedges for garnish

Drain oil from tuna and turn onto plate lined with salad greens. Arrange potato salad, cucumber, radishes, carrot, olives, onion, and egg around tuna. Combine capers and mayonnaise. Serve with caper-mayonnaise and lemon.

Makes 2 servings.

For a buffet, simply increase ingredients. Tuna packed in larger sizes (6½ or 7 ounces, 9¼ ounces, 12½ or 13 ounces) would be more practical.

## Molded Salmon Salad

1 can (1 pound) salmon
1 tablespoon plain gelatin
¼ cup cold water
2 eggs, beaten
¾ teaspoon salt
½ cup chopped celery

1 teaspoon grated onion
¼ cup lemon juice
¼ cup water
Lettuce
Mayonnaise or salad dressing

Drain and flake salmon. Soften gelatin in cold water 5 minutes. Combine eggs, salt, celery, onion, lemon juice, and remaining water. Cook until thick, stirring constantly. Add gelatin; stir until dissolved. Add salmon and pour into a mold; chill until firm. Unmold on lettuce. Garnish and serve with mayonnaise.

Makes 6 servings.

# Creamy Salmon Mold

1 can (15½ ounces or 439 grams)
    salmon
½ cup mayonnaise
¼ cup chopped cucumber
1 tablespoon unflavored gelatin

⅓ cup cold water
1 cup chicken broth
1 tablespoon lemon juice
3 drops liquid hot pepper sauce
Lettuce

Drain and flake salmon, reserving liquid. Either pink or red salmon may be used. Combine salmon, mayonnaise, and cucumber. Soften gelatin in cold water. Add hot chicken broth, stirring to dissolve gelatin. Add reserved salmon liquid, lemon juice, and liquid hot pepper sauce. Cool until partially set. Beat into salmon mixture. Place in an oiled 4-cup mold. Refrigerate until firm. Turn mold out onto lettuce lined platter. Garnish with parsley or dillweed if desired.

Makes 6 servings.

# Mullet Macaroni Salad

2 cups cooked, flaked mullet
2 cups cooked shell macaroni
1 cup raw cauliflower
1 cup sliced celery
¼ cup chopped parsley
¼ cup chopped sweet pickle or
    drained pickle relish
½ cup mayonnaise or salad
    dressing

3 tablespoons garlic French
    dressing*
1 tablespoon lemon juice
1 teaspoon grated onion
1 teaspoon celery seed
½ teaspoon pepper
Salad greens
1 hard-cooked egg, sliced

Combine mullet, macaroni, cauliflower, celery, parsley, and pickle. Combine mayonnaise, French dressing, lemon juice, onion, and seasonings; mix thoroughly. Add mayonnaise mixture to mullet mixture and toss lightly; chill. Serve on salad greens. Garnish with egg slices.

Makes 6 servings.

*If garlic French dressing is not available, use 3 tablespoons regular French dressing and add ⅛ teaspoon garlic juice to dressing.

## Tantalizing Mullet Salad

2 cups cooked, flaked mullet
¾ cup sliced celery
½ cup sliced green onion
3 tablespoons cider vinegar
2 tablespoons cooking oil
2 tablespoons soy sauce

1 tablespoon water
2 teaspoons mayonnaise
1 teaspoon sugar
⅛ teaspoon ground ginger
Dash pepper
Salad greens

Combine fish, celery, and green onions. Combine vinegar, cooking oil, soy sauce, water, mayonnaise, sugar, ginger, and pepper in a blender and mix until smooth. Pour over fish mixture. Chill at least 1 hour. Serve on salad greens.

Makes 5 servings.

## Smokey Mullet Dinner Salad

½ pound smoked mullet
1 cup mayonnaise or salad dressing
1 teaspoon prepared mustard
½ teaspoon tarragon leaves
½ teaspoon salt
¼ teaspoon celery seed

3 cups chilled, sliced, cooked
   potatoes
⅔ cup sliced celery
⅔ cup sliced radishes
⅓ cup sliced green onions
Lettuce leaves

Remove skin and bones from fish. Flake the fish. Combine mayonnaise, mustard, tarragon leaves, salt, and celery seed. Mix well. Fold in sliced potatoes. Add celery, radishes, onion, and flaked fish; mix carefully. Cover; refrigerate several hours to blend flavors. Arrange in center of a lettuce-lined serving dish; garnish with additional sliced smoked mullet.

Makes 6 servings.

# King Kabob Salad

*Fishing in the icy waters of the North Pacific is a dangerous enterprise. The long winters are marked by winds of one hundred knots, while the summers are known for their violent storms. Fishing in such conditions requires great skill and hardiness. This is particularly true of the seamen on the king crab fleet, who routinely haul huge traps, called "pots," holding one thousand pounds of king crab aboard ships on rough seas.*

| | |
|---|---|
| 8 ounces king crab leg meat, fresh or frozen | 8 ripe olives, pitted |
| Salad greens | 4 hard-cooked eggs, quartered |
| 1 quart shredded salad greens | 1 lemon, quartered |
| 16 cucumber chunks, cut into ¾-inch pieces | 4 sweet-pickle fans |
| 16 cherry tomatoes | Parsley sprigs |
| | Thousand Island dressing |

Thaw crab if frozen. Cut into ¾-inch pieces. Line four salad plates with salad greens; fill with shredded salad greens. Alternate on each of 8 skewers crabmeat, cucumber, tomato, and olive. Place 2 skewers on each plate on top of shredded lettuce. Garnish with one egg, quartered; 1 lemon wedge, 1 pickle fan, and parsley sprig. Serve with Thousand Island dressing.

Makes 4 servings.

# Green Goddess Shrimp Salad

*Green Goddess Salad was created in San Francisco in 1915 to honor George Arliss, who was starring in the play* The Green Goddess. *Combined with Pacific shrimp the salad, which boasts a unique dressing, becomes a main dish that is an excellent luncheon choice.*

1 pound cooked, peeled, deveined Pacific shrimp or other small shrimp, fresh or frozen

1¼ cups mayonnaise or salad dressing

1 can (2 ounces) or 2 tablespoons anchovy fillets, drained and chopped

2 tablespoons chopped parsley

2 tablespoons chopped chives or green onions and tops

2 tablespoons tarragon vinegar

1 small clove garlic, minced

About 3 quarts romaine lettuce, crisped, torn into bite-sized pieces

Thaw shrimp if frozen. Combine mayonnaise, anchovy, parsley, chives, vinegar, and garlic; blend flavors for several hours. Makes about 1½ cups dressing. Toss half the dressing (¾ cup) with romaine. Place about 2 cups of salad mixture on each of six salad plates; portion shrimp equally on top of salads. Spoon remaining salad dressing over shrimp if desired. Note that this dressing keeps well in refrigerator for later use.

Makes 6 servings.

## Lobster Salad

*An early reference to Lobster Salad can be found in the first Texas cookbook. Published in Houston in 1883 by the women of the First Presbyterian Church, the recipe was a favorite of the day and remains a popular dish a century later.*

1 pound cooked spiny lobster meat, fresh or frozen

6 hard-cooked eggs

½ cup salad oil

1 tablespoon sugar

1 teaspoon dry mustard

1 teaspoon salt

¼ teaspoon cayenne pepper

½ cup vinegar

1½ cups chopped celery

1½ cups chopped green onion

2 tablespoons capers with liquid

Salad greens

Thaw lobster meat if frozen. Cut meat into ½-inch cubes. Peel eggs; separate whites and yolks. Sieve or mash the egg yolks; gradually blend in oil. Stir sugar, mustard, salt, and pepper into vinegar. Combine with egg yolks. Set aside. Chop egg whites. Combine lobster meat, celery, egg whites, green onion, and capers. Pour dressing over salad and mix lightly. Serve on salad greens.

Makes 6 servings.

# Crab Louis

1 pound Dungeness crabmeat, or
    other crabmeat, fresh, frozen,
    or pasteurized
½ pound Dungeness or king crab
    legs or other crab legs, fresh or
    frozen
Salad greens
1½ quarts shredded salad greens
1 cup mayonnaise or salad
    dressing
2 tablespoons finely chopped
    green pepper

2 tablespoons finely chopped
    onion
2 tablespoons finely chopped
    parsley
¼ cup chili sauce
⅛ teaspoon cayenne pepper
¼ cup whipping cream, whipped
2 hard-cooked eggs, quartered
2 tomatoes, quartered
Ripe olives
Parsley sprigs
Lemon wedges

Thaw crabmeat if frozen. Drain crabmeat. Remove any remaining pieces of shell or cartilage. Line salad plates or bowls with salad greens; fill with shredded salad greens. Mound body crabmeat on lettuce. Combine mayonnaise, green pepper, onion, parsley, chili sauce, and cayenne. Fold in whipped cream. Pour sauce over crabmeat. Garnish plates with crab legs, eggs, tomatoes, olives, parsley, and lemon wedges.

Makes 4 servings.

# Sea 'n' Ranch Salad

*California is the birthplace of the tuna industry, and is the home port for much of the fishing fleet. Due to the variety of its climate and land, the state has also contributed many food commodities such as avocados, oranges, and walnuts. California is a rich, bounteous state and the Sea 'n' Ranch Salad pays tribute to its fruitfulness.*

1 can (6½ or 7 ounces) tuna
¼ cup mayonnaise
1 teaspoon dry mustard
½ cup chopped celery
¼ cup chopped walnuts
1 hard-cooked egg, chopped
½ teaspoon salt

⅛ teaspoon pepper
1 large head iceberg lettuce
1 avocado, sliced lengthwise
1 orange, peeled and sliced
¼ cup sliced onion, separated into
    rings
Chopped parsley

Drain tuna. Blend mayonnaise and mustard. Combine mayonnaise mixture, tuna, celery, walnuts, egg, salt, and pepper. Remove 4 large leaves from head of lettuce; shred remaining lettuce. Line each serving plate with a lettuce leaf; fill with a bed of shredded lettuce. Top with avocado slices and a scoop of tuna mixture. Garnish with orange slices and onion rings. Sprinkle with parsley.

Makes 4 servings.

## Polynesian Rock Shrimp Salad

1 pound cooked, peeled, and deveined rock shrimp
1 can (8 ounces) unsweetened
pineapple chunks
2 tablespoons reserved pineapple
juice
1 cup thinly sliced celery
½ cup seedless green grape halves
¼ cup sliced green onion

2 tablespoons mayonnaise or
salad dressing
2 tablespoons dairy sour cream
2 to 3 drops liquid hot pepper
sauce
½ teaspoon salt
Dash white pepper
Salad greens
Paprika

Cut large rock shrimp in half. Drain pineapple, being sure to reserve 2 tablespoons of juice. Combine rock shrimp, pineapple, celery, grape halves, and green onion in a medium-sized bowl. Combine pineapple juice, mayonnaise or salad dressing, sour cream, liquid hot pepper sauce, salt, and white pepper; mix well. Pour over rock shrimp mixture and toss lightly. Chill for at least 30 minutes. Serve on salad greens. Sprinkle with paprika.

Makes 4 to 6 servings.

## Easy Tuna Coleslaw

1 pound shredded cabbage
½ cup Thousand Island dressing

1 can (9¼ ounces) tuna in vegetable oil

Mix all ingredients thoroughly.

Makes 4 servings.

## Tuna Salad Filled Tomatoes

½ cup mayonnaise
1 teaspoon prepared mustard
1 tablespoon lemon juice
2 cans (6½ or 7 ounces each) tuna
    in vegetable oil

1 cup diced celery
4 tomatoes
Salad greens
¼ cup toasted slivered almonds

Blend mayonnaise, mustard, and lemon juice. Add tuna and celery; toss lightly. Cut tomatoes in sixths "petal fashion"; fill centers with the tuna salad. Serve on salad greens and garnish with toasted almonds.

Makes 4 servings.

## Smokey Seafood Salad

1½ pounds smoked mullet or
    other smoked fish
6 cups salad greens
1½ cups drained cooked peas
1 cup Swiss cheese, cut julienne
    style
1 cup red onion rings, sliced thin

⅓ cup mayonnaise or salad
    dressing
1 tablespoon sugar
¾ teaspoon salt
¼ teaspoon pepper
¼ cup cooked crumbled bacon
6 cherry tomatoes

Remove skin and bones from fish. Flake the fish. Combine salad greens, peas, cheese, onion, and fish. Combine mayonnaise, sugar, salt, and pepper. Chill before serving. Pour dressing over salad. Toss lightly and sprinkle with bacon. Garnish with cherry tomatoes.

Makes 6 servings.

## Plantation Fish in Aspic

*According to legend, in the 1700s a man named John Rutledge decided to run for office in a district near Charleston. To bolster his campaign effort he staged a feast on the lawn of the Rutledge*

*Plantation for people from miles around. The menu included such fare as venison, roast oysters, shrimp, fish in aspic, salads, and, of course, a variety of spirits. Some say that the following recipe for fish in aspic may be similar to the one used at the Rutledge campaign feast.*

2 pounds grouper or other fish fillets, fresh or frozen
2 cups boiling water
1 cup sauterne wine
1 medium onion, quartered
1 stick celery, quartered
2 bay leaves
1½ teaspoons salt
¼ teaspoon dried thyme leaves, crushed
1 lemon
½ cup cold water
2 tablespoons unflavored gelatin
¼ cup tarragon vinegar
2 tablespoons lemon juice
1 teaspoon dry mustard
¼ cup chopped celery
¼ cup chopped green onion
¼ cup chopped green pepper
2 tablespoons chopped pimiento
2 tablespoons chopped parsley
Salad greens
Mayonnaise

Thaw fish if frozen. Place in a well-greased 10-inch fry pan. Add 2 cups boiling water, wine, onion, celery, bay leaves, salt, and thyme. Cut lemon in half, squeeze in juice, and drop in halves. Cover and simmer for 5 to 10 minutes or until fish flakes easily when tested with a fork. Remove fish; set aside to cool. Strain poaching liquid. In a 4-cup measure, place ½ cup cold water. Stir in gelatin to soften. Add hot poaching liquid; stir to dissolve gelatin. Add vinegar, lemon juice, and enough water to make 4 cups liquid. Make a paste of dry mustard with small amount of the liquid; stir into remaining liquid. Chill to unbeaten egg white consistency. Remove skin and bones from fish. Flake fish into small pieces. Mix together fish, celery, green onion, green pepper, pimiento, and parsley. Fold together fish mixture and gelatin. Turn into a lightly oiled loaf pan, 9 × 5 × 3 inches, or a 7-cup mold. Chill until firm. Unmold on a serving dish lined with salad greens. Serve with mayonnaise.

Makes 6 servings.

# Clam Potato Salad

1 pint fresh clams or 2 cans (7
    ounces each) clams
2 tablespoons butter or other fat
1 cup diced cooked potatoes
2 hard-cooked eggs, chopped
1 cup chopped celery
1 tablespoon grated onion

2 tablespoons chopped pimiento
1 teaspoon salt
Dash pepper
¼ teaspoon thyme
½ cup mayonnaise or salad
    dressing
Lettuce cups

Drain clams and cook in butter until the edges curl. Chop. Combine all ingredients except lettuce; chill. Serve on lettuce cups.

Makes 6 servings.

# Razor Clam Aspic

1 can (7 ounces) minced razor
    clams
1 tablespoon plain gelatin
¼ cup cold water
½ cup water
½ cup clam liquor

½ cup chopped celery
¼ cup chopped stuffed olives
½ teaspoon Worcestershire sauce
Mayonnaise or salad dressing
Lettuce

Soften gelatin in the ¼ cup cold water 5 minutes. Heat clams, remaining water, and clam liquor. Add gelatin and stir until dissolved; cool. Add vegetables and seasonings. Pour into 6 individual molds. Chill until firm. Unmold on lettuce. Garnish and serve with mayonnaise.

Makes 6 servings.

## Seafood Tomato Aspic

1 cup crabmeat, shrimp, or flaked
    cooked fish
2 tablespoons plain gelatin
¼ cup cold water
2 bouillon cubes
1 teaspoon onion juice
¼ bay leaf

1½ cups boiling water
1 can (6 ounces) tomato paste
½ cup celery, chopped
Salad greens
Whipped Cream Dressing, see
    below

Soften gelatin in cold water 5 minutes. Add bouillon cubes, onion juice, and bay leaf to boiling water; simmmer 10 minutes. Add gelatin and stir until dissolved. Stir in tomato paste; cool. Add seafood and celery; pour into mold. Chill until firm. Unmold on salad greens. Garnish and serve with Whipped Cream Dressing.

Makes 6 servings.

## Whipped Cream Dressing

½ cup whipping cream
½ teaspoon salt

2 tablespoons mayonnaise or salad
    dressing

Whip cream until stiff. Fold in salt and mayonnaise. Chill. Serve with molded fish salads.

Makes 6 servings.

# Main Dishes—Fish

# Broiled Salmon Steaks
# with Currant-Lemon Barbecue Sauce

6 salmon or halibut steaks, ¾ to
    1 inch thick
½ cup lemon juice
¼ cup currant jelly
¼ cup corn syrup

¼ cup margarine or butter
3 tablespoons catsup
1 tablespoon prepared mustard
1 teaspoon cornstarch
1 teaspoon salt

Thaw steaks if frozen. Place fish in a single layer in a shallow baking dish. Brush steaks on both sides with lemon juice, cover, and refrigerate for 2 hours before broiling. Just before broiling steaks prepare sauce. Combine remaining lemon juice, jelly, syrup, margarine or butter, catsup, mustard, and cornstarch in sauce pan; stir until free of lumps. Cook until thickened, stirring constantly. Simmer 1 to 2 minutes. Cook in open broiler or over an open fire as follows:

### To Broil in Open Broiler

Drain steaks, sprinkle both sides with salt. Place fish in a single layer on a well-greased broiler pan. Brush fish with sauce. Broil about 3 to 4 inches from source of heat 4 to 6 minutes. Turn carefully and brush with sauce. Broil 4 to 6 minutes longer or until fish flakes easily when tested with a fork.

### To Cook over Open Fire

Drain steaks, sprinkle both sides with salt. Place fish in well-greased, hinged wire grills. Brush fish with sauce. Cook about 4 to 6 inches from moderately hot coals for 5 to 8 minutes. Baste with sauce. Turn and cook for 7 to 10 minutes longer or until fish flakes easily when tested with a fork. Serve with remaining sauce.

Makes 6 servings.

## Hawaiian Kabobs Teriyaki

*The Hawaiian islands are a mixture of various peoples, each with their customs and traditions. Many ethnic groups have contributed to the foods of Hawaii. The Chinese brought with them soy marinade, ginger, and the use of small pieces of food. From the Japanese came hibachi cooking, and from the Spanish came the pineapple. All of these elements are found in Hawaiian Kabobs Teriyaki.*

2 pounds cod fillets or other thick fish fillets, fresh or frozen
1 can (16 ounces) pineapple chunks
¼ cup reserved pineapple juice
½ cup soy sauce
¼ cup sherry, optional
2 tablespoons brown sugar

1 tablespoon freshly grated ginger root, or 1 teaspoon ground ginger
1 teaspoon dry mustard
1 clove garlic, crushed
1 green pepper, cut into 1-inch squares
3 cups cooked rice, optional

Thaw fish if frozen. Cut into 1-inch cubes. Drain pineapple; reserve ¼ cup of liquid. Combine pineapple juice, soy sauce, sherry, brown sugar, ginger, mustard, and garlic. Pour this marinade over the fish. Cover and refrigerate for at least one hour. Drain fish and reserve marinade. Thread fish, pineapple chunks, and green pepper alternately on skewers. Cook over hot coals or under a broiler, 4 to 5 inches from the source of heat, for 4 to 5 minutes or longer—until the fish flakes easily when tested with a fork. Serve as an entree on a bed of rice or alone as an appetizer. For an extra festive touch, place a flower on the end of each skewer after cooking.

Makes 6 servings.

## Sandy Bog Fillets

*The cranberry has a long history of use in America. The Indians used cranberries well before the arrival of the colonists, and it is generally thought that they introduced cranberries to the early settlers. Soon thereafter the colonists combined the cranberry with fish.*

2 pounds haddock fillets or other
    fish fillets, fresh or frozen
4 cups apple juice
1 rib celery, cut into 1-inch
    lengths

½ cup sliced onion
1 bay leaf
4 peppercorns
1 teaspoon salt
Cranberry Sauce, see below

Thaw fillets, if frozen. Cut into serving size portions. In a 10-inch skillet combine apple juice, celery, onion, bay leaf, peppercorns, and salt. Heat to boiling. Simmer for 10 minutes to blend flavors. Add fish and poach 4 to 5 minutes or until fish flakes easily when tested with a fork. Carefully remove fish to a hot platter. Reserve poaching liquid; strain. Pour Cranberry Sauce over fish.

Makes 6 servings.

## Cranberry Sauce

Reserved poaching liquid
2 cups fresh cranberries
¼ cup sugar

¼ cup lemon juice
¾ teaspoon cinnamon

Cook poaching liquid until it is reduced to 1 cup. Add cranberries, sugar, lemon juice, and cinnamon. Cook for approximately 5 minutes or until cranberry skins pop.

Makes 2 cups.

## About Dried Salt Codfish

*Drying fish was a commonly used method of preservation that dates back to medieval times. Later in history, salting fish finally became feasible on a large scale and gradually replaced dried fish in economic importance.*

*Fish are salted and then dried until their water content is reduced to less than 16 percent. This method produces a superior product for storage as well as imparting a unique flavor and texture. Nutritionally, one pound of dried salt codfish is equal to three and one-half pounds of fresh fish. No wonder that dried salt codfish became such a valuable commodity to our early colonists.*

*Canada, Iceland, Norway, and Newfoundland are the principal exporting countries with Newfoundland being the largest single source. Thanks to these countries, salt cod is available throughout the world and is readily obtainable for our culinary enjoyment.*

## Codfish Balls

1 pound dried salt codfish
2 cups mashed potatoes
2 eggs, well beaten
2 tablespoons grated onion

2 tablespoons chopped parsley,
    optional
Dash pepper
All-purpose flour

Soak codfish overnight. Drain. Simmer in water until tender; drain and flake. Mix codfish, potatoes, eggs, and seasonings together. Shape into small balls and roll in flour. Fry in deep fat, 375 degrees F., 3 to 5 minutes or until golden brown.

Makes 6 servings.

## Cape Cod Turkey with Egg Sauce

*The traditional "bird" of Thanksgiving on Cape Cod is not turkey. It is codfish. Served with egg sauce, codfish is delicious seafood fare.*

2 pounds cod fillets or other fish
    fillets, fresh or frozen
1 teaspoon salt
¼ teaspoon pepper
2 tablespoons melted margarine or
    butter
4 cups fresh bread crumbs
2 tablespoons melted margarine or
    butter

2 tablespoons grated onion
2 teaspoons dillweed
2 teaspoons chopped parsley
1 teaspoon leaf thyme
½ teaspoon salt
Dash pepper
2 eggs, beaten
Egg Sauce, see Sauces chapter
Sliced egg

Thaw fish if frozen. Sprinkle with salt and pepper. Place half the fillets in a well-greased baking dish 12 × 8 × 2 inches. Combine bread crumbs, 2 tablespoons margarine, onion, dillweed, parsley, thyme, salt, pepper, and eggs. Mix well. Spread on top of fillets in baking dish. Use remaining fillets and place on top of stuffing. Brush with 2 tablespoons melted margarine. Bake in a moderate oven, 350 degrees F., for 35 to 40 minutes or until fish flakes easily when tested with a fork. Serve fish with Egg Sauce. Garnish with sliced egg.

Makes 6 to 8 servings.

# Philadelphia Harborside Hash

*In the past women would often cook potatoes and bits of meat to mix with cooked fish to make a hash. The hash, which was a hearty dish, could be served for any meal. Philadelphia Harborside Hash is a variation of some of those early recipes.*

2 cups cooked, flaked haddock or
    other fish, fresh or frozen
3 slices bacon, diced
1 cup chopped onion
4 cups cooked, diced potatoes

1½ teaspoons salt
¼ teaspoon pepper
⅛ teaspoon cayenne
Vinegar, optional

Thaw fish if frozen. In a large skillet cook bacon until partially done. Add onion and continue to cook until done. Stir in potatoes, fish, salt, pepper, and cayenne. Spread hash evenly over bottom of skillet and cook until bottom is browned and crusty. Turn mixture and continue to cook until browned. Serve with vinegar, if desired.

Makes 4 to 6 servings.

# Cod Stuffed Potatoes

*The white potato was introduced to our country from South America sometime in the eighteenth century, but it was not until after 1800 that it came into prominent use. Maine offers an ideal climate for potatoes, and it was only a question of time before the Maine potato and the Massachusetts codfish were combined to make a tasty and unique dish.*

1½ pounds skinless codfish fillets
    or other fish fillets, fresh or
    frozen
2 cups boiling water
1 teaspoon salt
6 medium baking potatoes,
    cooked
1 cup hot milk
¼ cup margarine or butter

1½ tablespoons grated onion
1½ tablespoons chopped parsley
1½ teaspoons dry mustard
1½ teaspoons salt
¼ teaspoon pepper
Bacon drippings
Paprika
Pork Sauce, see below

Thaw fish if frozen. Place fish in a well-greased 10-inch fry pan. Add boiling water and salt. Cover and simmer for 5 to 10 minutes or until fish flakes easily when tested with a fork. Remove fish from liquid and flake. Reserve 1½ cups liquid for Pork Sauce. Cut a slice off the top of each potato; scoop out potatoes and mash. Stir in milk, margarine, onion, parsley, mustard, salt, and pepper. Stir in flaked fish. Stuff potato shells with potato-fish mixture. Drizzle with reserved bacon drippings from sauce. Sprinkle with paprika. Bake in a moderate oven, 350 degrees F., for 25 to 30 minutes or until hot. Serve Pork Sauce over potatoes.

Makes 6 servings.

# Pork Sauce

¼ pound bacon or salt pork,
    minced
¼ cup all-purpose flour

½ teaspoon salt
1½ cups reserved fish liquid
1 cup milk

In a small saucepan cook bacon until browned. Remove bacon; drain and reserve. Reserve 2 tablespoons bacon drippings in saucepan and reserve remaining drippings to put over stuffed potatoes. To drippings in saucepan blend in flour and salt. Gradually add fish liquid and milk. Cook until thick. Stir in reserved bacon.

Makes approximately 2½ cups.

## New Bedford Walnut Fried Flounder

*When the settlers first came to New England, they learned much from the Indians about the native foods, particularly nuts and berries. It was only natural that the early colonists would incorporate many of the Indian foods into their cooking.*

| | |
|---|---|
| 2 pounds flounder fillets or other fish fillets, fresh or frozen | 1 teaspoon marjoram leaves |
| 1 teaspoon salt | ½ teaspoon leaf thyme |
| ¼ teaspoon pepper | 1 cup all-purpose flour |
| 1½ cups fresh bread crumbs | 2 eggs, beaten |
| 1½ cups ground walnuts | ⅓ cup margarine or butter |
| 1½ teaspoons crushed rosemary | ⅓ cup cooking oil |
| | Lemon wedges |

Thaw fish if frozen. Sprinkle with salt and pepper. Combine bread crumbs, walnuts, rosemary, marjoram, and thyme. Roll fillets in flour, dip in egg, and roll in crumb mixture. Heat margarine and oil in a fry pan until hot, but not smoking. Place fish in pan and fry at a moderate heat for 4 to 5 minutes or until browned. Turn carefully and fry 4 to 5 minutes longer or until fish is browned and flakes easily when tested with a fork. Drain on absorbent paper. Serve with lemon wedges.

Makes 6 servings.

## New Bedford Flounder Roll-Ups

| | |
|---|---|
| 4 pounds flounder fillets | 8 cups instant mashed potatoes, prepared |
| 1 bud garlic | |
| 12 slices bacon | |

If fillets are frozen, defrost. Rinse and dry. Split fillets into serving pieces. Rub each fillet with crushed garlic. Roll; wrap bacon around fillet and skewer. Place in each of 12 au gratin dishes ⅔ of a cup of mashed potatoes. Top with fillet and broil until bacon and fillet are brown. Turn 2 or more times while broiling, about 10 minutes.

Makes 12 servings.

# Sourdough Fried Fish with Blueberry Sauce

*Sourdough starter was a mainstay of the early Alaskan settlers. Using it with flour and salt they made bread, biscuits, and flap-jacks, as well as an excellent coating for fried fish. The fish is particularly tasty when served with Blueberry Sauce.*

### Sourdough Starter

1 package active dry yeast  
1 quart lukewarm water

2 tablespoons sugar  
4 cups all-purpose flour

In a large crock or mixing bowl, soften yeast in water. Add sugar and flour; beat until ingredients are blended. Cover and let rise. Let stand at room temperature several days to develop slightly sour flavor; refrigerate. As starter is used, add equal amounts of flour and water to replace the amount used. The starter will need additions of flour and water about once a week if not used.

### Sourdough Fried Fish

#### Step 1

½ cup sourdough starter  
1 cup lukewarm water

1¼ cups all-purpose flour

#### Step 2

¼ cup milk or cream  
1 egg, beaten  
1 tablespoon sugar

1 tablespoon vegetable oil  
½ teaspoon baking soda  
½ teaspoon salt

#### Step 3

2 pounds lingcod fillets, or other thick fish fillets, fresh or frozen  
1 teaspoon salt

¼ teaspoon pepper  
½ cup all-purpose flour  
Fat for frying  
Blueberry Sauce, see below

Mix ingredients in Step 1. Cover and let stand overnight; place fish, if frozen, in refrigerator to thaw. When ready to cook, stir ingredients in Step 2 into refrigerated batter. Let stand and bubble 10 minutes.

Step 3: Cut fish into serving-size portions and sprinkle with salt and pepper; coat with flour. Dip fish in sourdough batter. Fry in large, deep skillet with fat approximately 2 inches deep, turning once until both sides are brown and fish flakes easily when tested with a fork. Drain on absorbent paper. Serve with hot Blueberry Sauce.

### Blueberry Sauce

2 cups blueberries
½ cup water
¼ to ⅓ cup sugar
2-inch stick cinnamon

2 tablespoons fresh lemon juice
1 teaspoon cornstarch
1 tablespoon water

In a saucepan combine blueberries, water, sugar, and cinnamon. Heat to simmering, stirring until sugar is dissolved; simmer 5 minutes. Stir in lemon juice. Blend cornstarch and water together. Add to sauce, stirring constantly. Heat to boiling, stirring constantly. Boil 2 minutes. Makes 1¾ cups sauce.

Makes 6 servings.

# Bake Sole Gourmet

2 pounds skinless sole fillets or
    other fish fillets, fresh or
    frozen
1 teaspoon salt
Dash pepper
1 package (10 ounces) frozen aspar-
    agus spears
1 tablespoon lemon juice

1 can (10½ ounces) cream of celery
    soup
1 teaspoon Worcestershire sauce
2 tablespoons grated Parmesan
    cheese
2 tablespoons toasted, blanched,
    slivered almonds

Thaw frozen fillets. Cut fillets into 6 portions. Sprinkle fish with salt and pepper. Cook asparagus according to directions on package. Place asparagus spears on fish. Roll fish around asparagus. Place fish in a well-greased baking dish, 12 × 8 × 2 inches. Combine lemon juice, soup, and Worcestershire sauce. Pour sauce over fish. Sprinkle with cheese and almonds. Bake in a moderate oven, 350 degree F., for 20 to 25 minutes or until fish flakes easily when tested with a fork.

Makes 6 servings.

# Diamond Jim Flounder

*Diamond Jim Brady is a legendary figure of early Manhattan. Stories about his enormous appetite for seafood abound, and it was said that fishermen would reserve their prize catches for him. The following recipe is a variation of one of Diamond Jim's favorites.*

## Poaching Stock

1½ pounds fish fillets, fresh or frozen (any inexpensive fish may be used)
1½ quarts water
2 medium onions, quartered

1 cup sliced carrots
8 peppercorns
1 bay leaf
¼ teaspoon leaf thyme

Thaw fillets if frozen. Cut into 1-inch cubes. In a large skillet combine water, onions, carrots, peppercorns, bay leaf, and thyme. Bring mixture to a boil and simmer for 5 minutes to blend flavors. Add fish cubes and let simmer until liquid is reduced to 2 cups. Strain through a cheesecloth. Reserve stock.

## Baked Fillets of Flounder

2 pounds flounder fillets, or other fish fillets, fresh or frozen
1 teaspoon salt
¼ teaspoon pepper
1 cup Poaching Stock

18 shucked, raw oysters
18 peeled, deveined shrimp
Marguery Sauce
Paprika

Thaw fish if frozen. Cut fillets into serving size portions. Sprinkle with salt and pepper. Place fish, oysters, and shrimp in a well-greased baking dish, 12 × 8 × 2 inches. Pour 1 cup Poaching Stock over fillets, oysters, and shrimp. Bake in a moderate oven, 350 degrees F., for 15 to 20 minutes, basting occasionally, until fish flakes easily when tested with a fork. Remove fish carefully to a broiling tray or ovenproof platter. Arrange 3 poached oysters and 3 poached shrimp on top of each serving. Keep warm. Cover with Marguery Sauce. Broil about 4 inches from source of heat until delicately browned. Sprinkle with paprika.

Makes 4 to 6 servings.

*Marguery Sauce*

1 cup Poaching Stock, plus pan
   juices from baking fillets,
   shrimp, and oysters
1 cup margarine or butter

8 egg yolks, beaten
2 tablespoons lemon juice
¼ cup dry white wine

In saucepan combine Poaching Stock and pan juices. Cook until volume of liquid is reduced to ½ cup. Add margarine and heat until melted. Beat in egg yolks with a wire whisk. Continue heating and beating until sauce thickens. Stir in lemon juice and mix well. Add wine; heat until hot enough to serve.

Makes about 2 cups.

# Sole Fillets Thermidor

3 pounds sole fillets or other thin
   fish fillets, fresh or frozen
1 (8 ounce) salmon fillet
⅛ teaspoon pepper
1½ teaspoons salt
2½ cups milk

½ cup margarine
½ cup all-purpose flour
½ pound (2 cups) mild Cheddar
   cheese, grated
½ cup lemon juice
Paprika

Thaw sole and salmon fillets if frozen. Cut sole fillets into 8 portions and salmon fillet into 8 equal pieces. Place a piece of salmon on each sole portion; sprinkle fish with pepper and 1 teaspoon salt; roll. Place fish rolls in a baking dish, 12 × 8 × 2 inches. Pour milk over rolls and bake in a moderate oven, 350 degrees F., for 30 minutes or until fish flakes easily when tested with a fork. Transfer fish rolls to deep ovenproof serving platter and keep warm. Reserve milk. In saucepan melt margarine, stir in flour and remaining ½ teaspoon salt. Add milk gradually and cook until thick and smooth, stirring constantly. Stir in cheese until melted; add lemon juice. Pour sauce over baked fish rolls. Sprinkle with paprika. Broil about 4 inches from source of heat for several minutes until lightly browned.

Makes 8 servings.

## Fish Muddle

1 pound haddock fillets or other
    fish fillets, fresh or frozen
1 pound ground pork sausage
1½ cups fresh bread crumbs
1 cup minced onion
1 egg, beaten
1 teaspoon marjoram leaves
½ teaspoon leaf thyme
⅛ teaspoon pepper

1 to 2 tablespoons cooking oil,
    optional
1 cup water
6 cups half and half
1½ teaspoons salt
½ cup instant mashed potato
    flakes
Chopped parsley
Chopped hard-cooked egg

Thaw fish if frozen. Cut fish into serving size portions. Combine sausage, bread crumbs, ½ cup minced onion, egg, marjoram, thyme, and pepper. Shape into balls using about 1 tablespoon mixture per ball. In a 5-quart Dutch oven brown meatballs adding 1 to 2 tablespoons cooking oil, if desired. Add ½ cup minced onion and continue to cook until onion is tender. Add water and bring to a boil. Cover and simmer for 10 to 15 minutes, or until meatballs are done. Place fish fillets on top of meatballs. Combine half and half, and salt. Pour over fish. Heat until fish flakes easily when tested with a fork. Stir in instant potatoes and heat for 2 to 3 minutes or until mixture is thick. Stir in chopped parsley. To serve, ladle into soup bowls; sprinkle with hard-cooked egg.

Makes 6 to 8 servings.

*Serving suggestion:* This is a delightful dish for a frosty night—serve with a nicely tossed salad and fresh, crusty French bread. Don't expect to have any leftovers.

## Oven-Fried Bluefish

2 pounds bluefish fillets or other
    fish fillets, fresh or frozen
1¼ teaspoons salt
¼ teaspoon pepper
1 cup instant mashed potato flakes

1 package (7/10 ounces) cheese-
    garlic salad dressing mix
1 egg, beaten
¼ cup butter or margarine, melted
Paprika

Thaw frozen fillets. Skin fillets. Cut fillets into serving size portions. Season fish with salt and pepper. Combine potato flakes and salad dressing mix. Dip fish into beaten egg and roll in potato mixture. Place fish in a single layer on a well-greased bake-and-serve platter, 16 × 10 inches. Pour melted butter or margarine over fish. Sprinkle with paprika. Bake in an extremely hot oven, 500 degrees F., for 10 to 12 minutes or until fish flakes easily when tested with a fork.

Makes 6 servings.

# Ceviche

*Living along the Pacific shores, the Indians of Central and South America enjoyed a land of abundance. The golden sun brought forth from the earth citrus trees, coriander, and chili peppers. The sea supplied fish in great variety and abundance. Taking advantage of these natural foods the Indians created ceviche centuries ago. When the Spanish came they adopted many of the Indian dishes and spread them throughout the new lands they explored.*

1 pound frozen sole fillets or other frozen skinned fillets
½ cup olive oil
½ cup salad oil
¼ cup chopped fresh coriander leaves* or 2 teaspoons coriander seeds, cracked
1 cup sliced pimiento-stuffed green olives

2 cups minced onion
⅔ cup lime juice
3 garlic cloves, minced
3 bay leaves
2 pickled jalapeño peppers, minced, or ½ teaspoon ground pepper
Shredded lettuce and chopped celery

Thaw fish. Cut fish into bite-size pieces, about one inch square. Mix olive oil, salad oil, and fresh coriander. If using coriander seeds, cook and stir seeds in a little of the oil 2 to 3 minutes over low heat; add remaining oil. Combine oil mixture, onion, olives, lime juice, garlic, bay leaves, and peppers. Pour marinade over fish and chill, covered, for two days before serving. Serve fish on a bed of shredded lettuce and chopped celery.

Makes 3 to 4 servings.

*The best place to find fresh coriander or cilantro is in Mexican markets or as Chinese parsley in Chinese markets.

## Petrale in the Classic Manner

*Many of the early California explorers and settlers were meat eaters and lacked appreciation for the Pacific's bountiful seafood. It was not until the arrival of the French, Orientals, and Italians that seafood began to be used in a variety of dishes.*

2 pounds sole fillets or other fish
    fillets, fresh or frozen
1 teaspoon salt
⅛ teaspoon pepper
¼ cup milk

½ cup all-purpose flour
6 tablespoons margarine or butter
6 tablespoons sliced almonds
2 tablespoons lemon juice
2 tablespoons chopped parsley

Thaw fish if frozen. Cut into serving size portions. Sprinkle with salt and pepper. Dip fish in milk and roll in flour. Melt margarine in a skillet and heat to a moderate temperature. Place fish in skillet. When fish is brown on one side, turn carefully and brown the other side. The cooking time is approximately 7 to 10 minutes depending on thickness of fish. Remove fish from pan and place on a hot platter. Add almonds to remaining margarine in pan and fry until lightly browned. Stir in lemon juice. Pour sauce over fish. Garnish with chopped parsley.

Makes 6 servings.

## Fillet of Sole Veronique

*Fillet of Sole Veronique comes down to us from some of the early French settlers. Having a knack for seafood cooking, they combined fish with grapes and wine to make a light, flavorful dish.*

2 pounds sole fillets or other fish
    fillets, fresh or frozen
2 tablespoons lemon juice
2 teaspoons salt
1 cup dry white wine
¼ teaspoon fines herbes

1 cup (¼ pound) white seedless
    grapes (If using canned
    grapes, do not poach grapes)
3 tablespoons margarine or butter
2 tablespoons all-purpose flour

Thaw fish if frozen. Cut into serving size portions. Sprinkle fillets with lemon juice and salt. Arrange in a well-greased 10-inch skillet in one or two layers. Combine wine, fines herbes, and grapes. Pour over fish and heat to simmering. Poach, covered, for about 5 minutes or until fish flakes easily when tested with a fork. Carefully remove sole, reserving liquid, and drain fish on absorbent paper. Transfer fish to oven-proof platter; strain grapes from liquid and save them for garnish. In separate pan, melt margarine and blend in flour. Add reserved liquid gradually and cook until thick and smooth, stirring constantly. Sauce should be light; add more wine if necessary. Pour sauce over fish and garnish with reserved grapes. Fish may be heated under the broiler until lightly browned.

### Shortcut Method

Poach fish and fresh grapes. Remove fish from poaching liquid and spread canned Hollandaise sauce over fish. Broil until hot and lightly browned. Garnish with reserved grapes.

Makes 4 servings.

## Dover Sole Sunriver

3 Dover sole, poached in 2 cups
   wine
3 hard-cooked eggs
½ pound boiled crawfish tails,
   minced
6 ounces white sauce, made with
   fish stock

½ pint whipped cream
2 ounces plain gelatin
Salt and pepper to taste
2 lemons, cut into wedges
1 bunch parsley

Combine crawfish, white sauce, and whipped cream. Season with salt and pepper to taste. Fold in softened gelatin. Coat sole with this mixture, chill, and decorate with additional sauce mixture. Halve the eggs, remove yolks, and fill with the sauce mixture. Arrange all on a platter and garnish with lemon wedges and parsley.

To make the white sauce from fish stock, melt 2 tablespoons of butter or margarine over low heat. Blend in 1½ tablespoons of all-purpose flour and stir over low heat for several minutes or until the taste of raw flour has vanished. Slowly stir in ¼ cup of milk or cream, and ½ cup fish stock. Simmer and stir with a wire whisk until thick and smooth.

Makes 3 to 6 servings.

# Fillet of Sole Florentine

24 pieces (4 pounds) fillet of sole
1½ cups seasoned bread stuffing
6 tablespoons melted butter or
    margarine

40 ounces frozen chopped spinach
1 cup cream
1½ teaspoons salt
¼ teaspoon pepper

If fillets are frozen, defrost. Rinse and dry. Cut fillets into portions. Prepare bread stuffing according to package directions. Spread on each fillet about 1 tablespoon dressing. Roll and skewer. Brush with butter or margarine. Place rolls on baking pan and broil until fish is done, about 10 to 12 minutes. Cook spinach and drain. Add cream, salt, and pepper. Place a layer of spinach in each hot, individual baking dish and arrange rolled fillets on top according to number of servings desired. For individual servings, 8 to 12 individual baking dishes will be required.

Makes 8 to 12 servings.

# Delmarvelous Bluefish

*During the second half of the nineteeth century Cape May, New Jersey was known as the Summer White House. Presidents Lincoln, Grant, Buchanan, and Harrison spent holidays there, enjoying the warm sun and cool, salt air. A favorite dish was bluefish, caught in local waters and baked in butter and wine.*

2 pounds bluefish fillets or other
    fish fillets, fresh or frozen
1 teaspoon salt
¼ teaspoon pepper

⅓ cup melted margarine or butter
3 tablespoons lemon juice
½ teaspoon thyme
Mustard Sauce, see below

Thaw fish if frozen. Cut into serving size portions. Sprinkle with salt and pepper. Put fish in a well-greased 2-quart baking dish. Combine margarine, lemon juice, and thyme. Pour over fish. Bake in a moderate oven, 350 degrees F., for 15 to 20 minutes or until fish flakes easily when tested with a fork. Serve with Mustard Sauce.

Makes 4 servings.

## Mustard Sauce

¼ cup margarine or butter
3 tablespoons all-purpose flour
1½ tablespoons dry mustard
½ teaspoon salt

¼ teaspoon liquid hot pepper
    sauce
2 cups half and half
1 egg yolk, beaten

In a saucepan melt margarine. Blend in flour, mustard, salt, and liquid hot pepper sauce. Gradually stir in half and half. Cook until thickened, stirring constantly. Add a little of the hot sauce to egg yolk; add to remaining sauce, stirring constantly. Heat until thickened. Serve sauce over fish.

Makes approximately 2 cups.

## Lemon Garlic Croaker

*When the French came to Louisiana, the women were faced with the problem of adapting traditional recipes to native ingredients. Soon, with the help of the Choctaw Indians, these women learned to use herbs, game, fish, and shellfish. They created many new dishes, variations of which are popular today.*

2 pounds croaker or other fish fil-
    lets, fresh or frozen
¼ cup lemon juice

1 teaspoon salt
1 clove garlic, minced
1½ cups cornmeal

Thaw fish if frozen. Combine lemon juice, salt, and garlic in shallow dish. Add fillets, turning them in lemon juice and placing them skinside up. Cover and place in refrigerator to marinate 30 minutes. Remove fish from marinade and roll in cornmeal. Place fish in heavy fry pan with melted margarine, hot but not smoking. Fry at a moderate heat. When fish is brown on one side, turn carefully and brown the other side. Cooking time is about 7 to 8 minutes, depending on thickness of fish. Drain on absorbent paper. Serve immediately on a hot platter.

Makes 6 servings.

## Baked Sea Bass, St. Helena

*It is a commonly held belief that white wine—and only white wine—enhances the flavor of fish. Baked Sea Bass, St. Helena dispels this misconception of white wine and fish by using a dry, red wine to bring out the flavor of a tasty gamefish.*

2 pounds sea bass fillets or other
    fish fillets, fresh or frozen
2 tablespoons lime juice
1 teaspoon salt
¼ teaspoon pepper
1 cup chopped onion
¼ cup margarine or butter, melted

1 bay leaf, crumbled
1 cup chopped fresh mushrooms
    or 1 can (4 ounces) sliced
    mushrooms, drained
½ cup dry red wine
2 tablespoons melted margarine or
    butter

Thaw fish if frozen. Cut into serving size portions. Sprinkle fish with lime juice, salt, and pepper. Cook onion in ¼ cup melted margarine until tender and spread into baking dish, 13×9×2 inches. Place fillets in a single layer on onion; add bay leaf and mushrooms to top of fish. Pour wine over fish and drizzle fillets with melted margarine. Basting frequently, bake in a hot oven, 400 degrees F., for 20 to 25 minutes or until fish flakes easily when tested with a fork. If desired, remove fish to hot serving platter after cooking; reduce or thicken pan juice and pour sauce over fish.

Makes 6 servings.

## Florida Red Snapper

*Various sections of the country specialize in particular fish industries. Alaska is known for its king crab, Massachusetts is famous for codfish, and Maine is often associated with lobster. Florida too is the center of a major fish industry—the red snapper, an excellent seafood dish.*

2 pounds red snapper fillets or
    other fish fillets, fresh or
    frozen
¼ cup grated onion
2 tablespoons orange juice

2 tablespoons lemon juice
2 teaspoons grated orange rind
½ teaspoon salt
⅛ teaspoon nutmeg
⅛ teaspoon pepper

Thaw fillets if frozen. Cut fish into 6 portions. Place in a single layer, skin-side down, in a well-greased baking dish, 12 × 8 × 2 inches. Combine onion, orange and lemon juice, orange rind, and salt. Pour over fish; cover and place in refrigerator to marinate 30 minutes. Sprinkle fish with nutmeg and pepper. Bake in a moderate oven, 350 degree F., for 25 to 30 minutes or until fish flakes easily when tested with a fork.

Makes 6 servings.

## Red Snapper with Vegetable Sauce

*Although the red snapper is usually found in semitropical or tropical waters, it has been known to swim as far north as Cape Hatteras. Its excellent taste has caused it to be in great demand. One of the outstanding red snapper recipes is to bake the fish with vegetable sauce.*

2 pounds red snapper fillets or other fish fillets, fresh or frozen
2 tablespoons olive oil
½ cup chopped onion
¼ cup chopped celery
¼ cup chopped green pepper
¼ cup sliced carrots
1 tablespoon chopped parsley

1 clove garlic, minced
1 can (15 ounces) tomato sauce with tomato bits
½ cup pale dry sherry
1 teaspoon dried dillweed
½ teaspoon salt
⅛ teaspoon pepper
1 tablespoon lemon juice

Thaw fish if frozen. Cut fish into 6 portions. In saucepan combine olive oil, onion, celery, green pepper, carrots, parsley, and garlic; cover and cook until tender. Stir in tomato sauce, sherry, and dillweed. Bring to a boil and simmer for 10 minutes. Ladle about ½ cup of the tomato-vegetable sauce into a 12 × 8 × 2-inch baking dish. Place fish portions on sauce in baking dish. Sprinkle with salt, pepper, and lemon juice. Pour remaining sauce over fish. Bake in a hot oven, 400 degrees F., for 20 to 25 minutes or until fish flakes easily when tested with a fork.

Makes 6 servings.

## Texas Grilled Spanish Mackerel

3 pounds dressed Spanish mackerel or other dressed fish, fresh or frozen
½ cup lemon juice
¼ cup olive oil
1 teaspoon salt

1 teaspoon dried oregano leaves, crushed
¾ teaspoon garlic salt
½ teaspoon pepper
½ teaspoon monosodium glutamate

Thaw fish if frozen. Combine lemon juice, olive oil, salt, oregano, garlic salt, pepper, and monosodium glutamate. Make 4 to 5 shallow slits on each side of each fish. Brush fish inside and outside with sauce. Place fish in well-greased, hinged, wire grills. Cook about 4 inches from moderately hot coals for 5 to 8 minutes. Baste with sauce. Turn. Cook for 5 to 8 minutes longer or until fish flakes easily when tested with a fork.

Makes 6 servings.

## King Mackerel Steaks with Sauce Provençale

*A favorite gamefish of the Gulf and South Atlantic is the king mackerel. They are fast and powerful and put up an excellent fight when hooked. They are also a delicious fish and hence they are the basis of many fine recipes.*

2 pounds king mackerel steaks, fresh or frozen
2 tablespoons melted margarine or butter

1 teaspoon salt
⅛ teaspoon pepper
Paprika
Sauce Provençale, see below

Thaw fish if frozen. Place fish in a single layer on a well-greased baking pan, 15 × 10 × 1 inches. Brush with margarine and sprinkle with salt, pepper, and paprika. Broil about 4 inches from source of heat for 10 to 15 minutes or until fish flakes easily when tested with a fork. Fish need not be turned during broiling. Serve with Sauce Provençale.

Makes 6 servings.

## Sauce Provençale

4 medium tomatoes, peeled, cut
    into wedges, and seeded
½ teaspoon sugar
2 tablespoons margarine or butter
¼ cup chopped green onion
1 clove garlic, minced

½ cup dry white wine
½ cup margarine or butter
2 tablespoons chopped parsley
¼ teaspoon salt
⅛ teaspoon pepper

Sprinkle tomatoes with sugar; set aside. In small saucepan melt 2 tablespoons margarine. Add green onion and garlic; cover and cook 2 to 3 minutes. Add wine. Cook, stirring constantly, until liquid is slightly reduced. Add tomatoes and remaining ingredients. Heat, stirring gently, just until margarine melts.

Makes 2 cups.

## Marinated King Mackerel, Norfolk Style

2 pounds king mackerel steaks, or
    other fish steaks, fresh or
    frozen
1 teaspoon dried marjoram leaves,
    crushed

¼ cup lime juice
2 tablespoons melted margarine or
    butter
1 teaspoon salt
⅛ teaspoon pepper

Thaw fish if frozen. Combine marjoram and lime juice in shallow dish. Add steaks, turning to moisten both sides with lime juice. Cover and place in refrigerator. Marinate 1 hour, turning once. Place fish in single layer on a well-greased baking pan, 15 × 10 × 1 inches. Brush fish with margarine. Sprinkle with salt and pepper. Broil about 4 inches from source of heat for 10 to 15 minutes or until fish flakes easily when tested with a fork. Fish need not be turned during broiling.

Makes 4 servings.

## Outer Banks Stuffed Spanish Mackerel

3 to 4 pounds dressed Spanish
    mackerel or other dressed
    fish, fresh or frozen
1½ teaspoons salt

¼ teaspoon pepper
Vegetable Stuffing, see below
2 tablespoons melted margarine or
    butter

Thaw fish if frozen. Clean, wash, and dry fish. Sprinkle inside and outside with salt and pepper. Place fish on a well-greased bake-and-serve platter, 18 × 13 inches. Stuff fish; brush with margarine. Bake in a moderate oven, 350 degrees F., for 30 to 45 minutes or until fish flakes easily when tested with a fork.

Makes 6 servings.

## Vegetable Stuffing

½ cup margarine or butter
1½ cups chopped onion
1 cup chopped celery
1 cup chopped fresh mushrooms
½ cup chopped green pepper

1 clove garlic, minced
2 tomatoes, peeled, seeded, and
    chopped
3 cups soft bread crumbs
½ teaspoon salt

In saucepan, melt margarine. Add onion, celery, mushrooms, green pepper, and garlic; cover and cook until tender. Combine all ingredients and mix well.

Makes 3½ cups.

## Atlantic City Flamed Sea Bass

*The sea bass is a favorite gamefish that can be cooked in a variety of ways—boiled, broiled, stewed, fried, or baked. The following recipe complements the sea bass's natural flavor.*

2 pounds sea bass fillets or other
    fish fillets, fresh or frozen
⅔ cup margarine or butter, melted
1 teaspoon paprika

1 bunch parsley
2 tablespoons fennel seed
½ cup brandy

Thaw fish if frozen. Divide into serving size portions. Place fish in a well-greased baking dish, 12 × 8 × 2 inches, with the skin side down. Combine margarine and paprika; brush fish with sauce. Reserve remaining sauce for serving with fish. Bake fish in a moderate oven, 350 degrees F., for 15 to 20 minutes or until fish flakes easily when tested with a fork. Cover serving platter with parsley; sprinkle fennel seed over parsley. Place fish on top of parsley. Pour reserved margarine mixture over fish. Heat brandy and flame; pour over fish.

Makes 6 servings.

## Portuguese Fisherman Stew

*Soon after the discovery of the New World, before the first settlements were established, Portuguese fishermen sailed the eastern coast of North America. From these fishermen came the fish stew, flavored with traditional ingredients such as herbs and garlic. It was inevitable that ingredients from the New World, including pumpkins and corn, were eventually added to these early stews.*

2 pounds striped bass fillets or
    other fish fillets, fresh or
    frozen
1 tablespoon margarine or butter
1 cup chopped onion
1 clove garlic, crushed
2 cans (1 pound each) tomatoes,
    undrained, cut up
3 cups water

1 teaspoon leaf basil
1 teaspoon leaf thyme
¼ teaspoon crushed red pepper
1 teaspoon salt
4 cups pumpkin or winter squash,
    cut into 1-inch cubes
2 ears corn, cut crosswise into
    1-inch pieces

Thaw fish if frozen. Cut fish into 1-inch cubes. In a large saucepan melt margarine. Add onion and garlic and cook until vegetables are tender. Add tomatoes, water, basil, thyme, red pepper, salt, pumpkin, and corn. Cover and bring to a boil; simmer for 10 to 15 minutes or until pumpkin and corn are done. Add fish and continue to cook for 5 to 10 minutes or until fish flakes easily when tested with a fork.

Makes 12 cups or 4 to 8 servings.

Any leftover stew may be frozen for future use.

## San Pedro Tuna Omelet

*When the Italians first settled in California, they brought with them artichokes. This vegetable is an important ingredient in San Pedro Tuna Omelet, a light dish ideal for lunch.*

2 cans (6½ or 7 ounces each) tuna, drained and flaked
2 cups half and half
2 tablespoons sliced green onion
½ teaspoon leaf thyme
½ teaspoon salt
6 or 8 drops liquid hot pepper sauce

2 tablespoons all-purpose flour
¼ cup water
¼ cup margarine or butter
12 eggs
1½ teaspoons salt
Dash pepper
1½ cups shredded Cheddar cheese

In a saucepan, heat tuna, half and half, onion, thyme, salt, and liquid hot pepper sauce until hot. Blend flour and water together. Add to sauce, stirring constantly, and cook until thick. For each omelet beat 2 eggs, ¼ teaspoon salt, and a dash of pepper together. To a small omelet pan add 2 teaspoons margarine and heat until margarine sizzles. Pour egg mixture into omelet pan. When eggs are partially cooked, run a spatula around the edge, lifting slightly to allow uncooked egg to flow underneath. When omelet is almost done, sprinkle ¼ cup cheese on top and continue to cook until cheese melts. Remove omelet to a hot platter. Repeat omelet procedure until 6 omelets are made. Place ½ cup tuna mixture on 1 side of each omelet. Fold omelets in half.

Makes 6 servings.

## Tuna Potato Scallop

2 cans (6½ to 7 ounces each) tuna
3 tablespoons butter or other fat
3 tablespoons all-purpose flour
½ teaspoon salt
Dash pepper
2 cups milk
4 cups cooked sliced potatoes

½ cup mayonnaise or salad dressing
½ cup grated cheese
1 teaspoon Worcestershire sauce
1 teaspoon prepared mustard
Dash paprika

Drain tuna. Break into large pieces. Melt butter; blend in flour and seasonings. Add milk gradually and cook until thick and smooth, stirring constantly. Add tuna. Arrange potatoes and tuna mixture in alternate layers in a well-greased baking pan, 11 × 7 × 1½ inches. Combine remaining ingredients and spread over the top. Bake in a moderate oven, 350 degrees F., for 30 minutes.

Makes 6 servings.

## Tuna and Corn Casserole

2 cans (6½ or 7 ounces each) tuna
½ cup chopped onion
¼ cup chopped green pepper
¼ cup butter or other fat, melted
1 package (8 ounces) macaroni
¾ cup milk

1 can (1 pound 4 ounces) cream
   style corn
¾ teaspoon salt
Dash pepper
Paprika

Drain tuna. Break into large pieces. Cook onion and green pepper in butter until tender. Cook macaroni as directed on package; drain. Combine all ingredients except paprika. Place in a well-greased, 2-quart casserole. Sprinkle with paprika. Bake in a moderate oven, 350 degrees F., for 50 minutes.

Makes 6 servings.

## Tuna Pot Pie

2 cans (6½ or 7 ounces each) tuna
1 cup cooked diced carrots
1 cup cooked peas
½ cup water

1 can (10½ ounces) condensed
   chicken soup or chicken
   broth
1 cup biscuit mix

Drain tuna. Break into large pieces. Combine carrots, peas, and tuna. Place in a well-greased, 1½-quart casserole. Combine water and soup, stirring until smooth; heat. Pour over tuna mixture. Prepare biscuit mix as directed. Drop by teaspoonfuls on top of the tuna mixture. Bake in a very hot oven, 450 degrees F., for 30 minutes or until brown.

Makes 6 servings.

## Tuna and Noodles Italian Style

2 cans (6½ or 7 ounces each) tuna
¾ cup chopped onion
½ cup chopped celery
1 clove garlic, finely chopped
¼ cup butter or other fat, melted
1 can (1 pound 13 ounces)
    tomatoes
½ cup water
1 can (6 ounces) tomato paste

1 tablespoon sugar
1½ teaspoons salt
Dash pepper
½ teaspoon whole oregano
1 teaspoon crushed sweet basil
1 whole bay leaf, crushed
1 package (8 ounces) noodles
2 cups grated cheese

Drain tuna. Break into large pieces. Cook onion, celery, and garlic in butter until tender. Add the next 9 ingredients and simmer for 1 hour. Add tuna and simmer for 5 minutes. Cook noodles as directed on package; drain. Arrange the noodles, tuna sauce, and cheese in alternate layers in a well-greased baking pan, 11 × 7 × 1½ inches. Bake in a moderate oven, 350 degrees F., for 35 to 40 minutes.

Makes 6 servings.

## Smoked Fish Cakes

1 pound smoked mullet or other
    smoked fish
½ cup chopped onion
2 tablespoons melted fat or oil
2 cups cold mashed potatoes

¼ cup chopped parsley
1 egg, beaten
Dash pepper
½ cup dry bread crumbs

Remove skin and bones from fish. Flake the fish. Cook onion in fat until tender. Combine all ingredients except crumbs. Shape fish mixture into 6 cakes and roll in crumbs. Fry in hot fat at moderate heat for 3 to 4 minutes or until brown. Turn carefully and fry 3 to 4 minutes longer or until brown. Drain on absorbent paper.

Makes 3 to 6 servings.

## Broiled Sesame Mullet

*Over the years Southern cooking has incorporated many African traditions. Sesame seeds are one of the most popular. Brought by the slaves who arrived in the South during the late seventeenth century, sesame seeds today are used in recipes throughout the country.*

2 pounds mullet fillets or other
    fish fillets, fresh or frozen
1 teaspoon salt
⅛ teaspoon pepper

¼ cup margarine or butter
2 tablespoons lemon juice
2 tablespoons toasted sesame
    seeds

Thaw fish if frozen. Cut into 6 portions. Place fish in a single layer, skin-side down, on a well-greased baking pan, 15 × 10 × 1 inches. Sprinkle with salt and pepper. Heat margarine and lemon juice together. Baste fish with sauce. Sprinkle with sesame seeds. Broil about 4 inches from source of heat for 10 to 15 minutes or until fish flakes easily when tested with a fork. Baste with any remaining sauce during cooking time. Fish need not be turned during broiling.

Makes 6 servings.

## Golden Halibut Bits

2 pounds halibut
1 cup dry pancake mix

¾ cup beer*

Cut halibut into 1½-inch pieces. Combine pancake mix with beer, and stir to blend. Dip halibut into batter and deep fry in hot oil, 375 degrees F., until golden brown, about 4 to 5 minutes. Drain and keep hot in oven while frying remai. 'ng halibut. Serve with French fried potatoes.

Makes 4 to 6 servings.

*For variation, substitute for beer with 1 cup milk and 1 well-beaten egg, or with ¾ cup buttermilk.

# Mullet Mobile

*Throughout the South sauces are considered an important element of good cooking. Many of these sauces come from the French, two favorites being Hollandaise and Béarnaise. Either one makes Mullet Mobile an extraordinary dish.*

2 pounds mullet fillets or other fish fillets, fresh or frozen
2 tablespoons melted margarine or butter
1 teaspoon salt
⅛ teaspoon pepper
Paprika
Hollandaise Sauce or Béarnaise Sauce, see Sauces chapter for easy blender sauces

Thaw fish if frozen. Cut fish into 6 portions. Place fish in a single layer, skin-side down, on a well-greased pan, 15 × 10 × 1 inches. Brush with margarine and sprinkle with salt, pepper, and paprika. Broil about 5 inches from source of heat for 10 to 15 minutes or until fish flakes easily when tested with a fork. Fish need not be turned during broiling. Serve with Hollandaise or Béarnaise Sauce.

Makes 6 servings.

# Halibut Corn Chowder

*New England is well known for its chowder, but coastal France also has a strong tradition for seafood dishes and chowders. Typically the chowders were combined with vegetables available at the time. When people from these areas migrated to America, they merely adapted their cooking habits to the New World, incorporating local ingredients in their recipes.*

2 pounds halibut fillets or steaks or other fish, fresh or frozen
4 slices bacon, diced
¾ cup chopped onion
2 cups diced potatoes
1½ cups water
1½ teaspoons salt
¼ teaspoon pepper
¼ teaspoon dillweed
1 can (16 ounces) cream style corn
2 cups half and half
2 cups milk
1½ tablespoons margarine or butter, softened
1½ tablespoons all-purpose flour
1 tablespoon chopped parsley

Thaw fish if frozen. Skin if desired and cut into 1-inch cubes. In a heavy kettle cook bacon until crisp. Add onion and cook until tender. Add potatoes, water, salt, pepper, and dillweed. Cover and simmer for 10 to 12 minutes or until potatoes are almost tender. Add fish and continue to simmer covered for 7 to 8 minutes or until fish flakes easily when tested with a fork. Add corn, half and half, and milk. Heat gently. Blend together margarine and flour. Add to chowder. Heat, stirring constantly, until thickened and hot enough to serve. Garnish with chopped parsley.

Makes 6 servings.

## Halibut Pot Roast

3 pounds halibut or other lean fish, in one piece
1 cup all-purpose flour
½ cup fat or oil
6 carrots
6 medium onions

2 cups chopped celery
6 medium potatoes
2 cloves garlic, finely chopped
2 teaspoons salt
½ teaspoon pepper
2 cups water

Remove skin and bones from fish. Roll fish in flour and brown in fat on all sides in a large heavy frying pan or Dutch oven. Place vegetables around fish and season with salt and pepper. Add water, cover, and bake in moderate oven, 350 degrees F., or until fish is done. Remove fish and vegetables to hot platter. Thicken liquid in pan and serve over fish and vegetables.

Makes 6 servings.

## Seafood Croquettes

2 cups flaked cooked seafood
1 cup grated cheese
2 eggs, well beaten
1 teaspoon salt

2 tablespoons lemon juice
2 tablespoons butter or other fat, melted
½ cup dry bread crumbs

Combine all ingredients except bread crumbs. Shape into 6 individual croquettes and roll in crumbs. Bake in a moderate oven, 350 degrees F., 25 to 30 minutes, or until brown. Serve plain or with a sauce.

Makes 6 servings.

# Fish Cakes, Smorgasbord

*American cooking has borrowed much from the traditions of other countries. The smorgasbord, so popular in America, can be traced to Sweden. In America the smorgasbord is usually served as a full course, including salads, main dishes, desserts, and coffee, while in Sweden it is usually presented as a cold first course. In either case the food is plentiful and one is encouraged to return for additional helpings.*

1 pound ocean perch fillets or
    other fish fillets, fresh or
    frozen
1 quart boiling water
1 teaspoon dill salt or 1 teaspoon
    salt and 1 teaspoon dill seed
2 cups mashed potatoes

⅓ cup grated onion
1 teaspoon salt
⅛ teaspoon white pepper
½ cup all-purpose flour
6 tablespoons margarine or butter
Smorgasbord Sauce, see below

Thaw fish if frozen. Place fillets in boiling water with dill salt or salt and dill seed. Cover and return to the boiling point. Reduce heat and simmer for about 5 minutes or until fish flakes easily when tested with a fork. Drain. Remove skin and bones; flake fish. Combine fish, potatoes, onion, salt, and pepper. Place flour on waxed paper. Shape fish mixture into 6 patties and roll in flour. Melt margarine in a 10-inch fry pan at a moderate temperature. Fry fish cakes in margarine for 2 to 3 minutes on each side. Drain on absorbent paper. Serve with Smorgasbord Sauce.

Makes 4 servings.

# Smorgasbord Sauce

⅓ cup cooking oil
⅓ cup chopped parsley
2 tablespoons Dijon-style mustard
2 teaspoons finely chopped sweet
    pickle

1 teaspoon lemon juice
1 teaspoon vinegar
1 teaspoon dillweed
½ teaspoon salt
¼ teaspoon pepper

Combine all ingredients and beat until creamy. This sauce keeps well and may be made ahead. It would be good served with almost any type fish.

Makes about 1 cup.

# Gulf Court Bouillon

*Gulf Court Bouillon is similar to bouillabaise although it shows a greater influence of Black and Indian traditions. This recipe results in a thickened sauce rather than a "soup," and may be served in individual serving dishes. The purpose of the soup bowl was to prevent the sauce from spilling onto the table. Any deeply lipped serving dish will do. However, most people prefer to serve Gulf Court Bouillon is soup bowls rather than purchase seldom used specialized dishes. Typical of Southern cooking, this recipe makes a hearty meal.*

2 pounds red drum fillets or
    steaks, or other fish fillets or
    steaks, fresh or frozen
⅓ cup cooking oil
½ cup all-purpose flour
1½ cups chopped onion
1 cup chopped celery
½ cup chopped green onion
½ cup chopped green pepper
2 tablespoons chopped parsley
1 clove garlic, minced
2 cans (15 ounces each) tomato
    sauce with tomato bits

¾ cup dry red wine
2 tablespoons lemon juice
½ teaspoon salt
½ teaspoon dried thyme leaves,
    crushed
¼ teaspoon dried marjoram
    leaves, crushed
¼ teaspoon cayenne pepper
6 whole allspice
1 bay leaf
Lemon slices

Thaw fish if frozen. Remove skin and bones from fish. Cut fish into 6 portions. In a heavy 4- to 5-quart Dutch oven, heat oil; blend in flour. Cook, stirring constantly, over medium heat until light brown in color, about 10 minutes. Add onion, celery, green onion, green pepper, parsley, and garlic. Cover and cook 5 minutes or until tender. Gradually stir in tomato sauce. Add wine, lemon juice, salt, thyme, marjoram, cayenne, allspice, and bay leaf. Bring to a boil and simmer for 30 minutes. Add fish to court bouillon. Cover and simmer 5 to 10 minutes or until fish flakes easily when tested with a fork. To serve, place portion of fish in soup bowl and pour about one cup sauce over fish. Garnish with lemon slices.

Makes 6 servings.

## Is Newburg really Newburg?

*On the serious side, Newburg is a rich cream and egg sauce in which seafood is served. It is usually flavored with sherry, but madeira or brandy is sometimes used. However, with a lot of luck and many laughs, another side of the story emerges—the "other" side.*

*In the midnineteenth century, a certain shipping magnate by the name of Mr. Wenburg was accustomed to eating at Delmonico's when in New York. On one occasion, he told the proprietor of a lobster dish he had enjoyed while in South America. Mr. Wenburg carefully described the rich creamy sauce as best he could, and the head chef prepared the dish. It quickly became a favorite and was placed on the menu officially as Lobster Wenburg.*

*Some time later, Mr. Wenburg engaged in a drunken brawl at the restaurant, causing considerable damage and embarrassment to the establishment. He was promptly escorted from the restaurant and his name was stricken from the menu. The popular lobster dish was still served, but the spelling was changed to disguise its ig- nominious origin. Thus, it became known as Lobster Newburgh. With time, however, the spelling was again changed so that by the late nineteenth century it became Lobster Newburg, the dish that we still appreciate today.*

## Perch Turbans à la Newburg

*When one thinks of New England and fish, Massachusetts usually comes to mind first. However, fish has been a major source of food for all of the New England states, starting with the original colonists. Early records of New Hampshire indicate that fish was so important to the local economy that payment was sometimes made in fish.*

| | |
|---|---|
| 2 pounds ocean perch or other fish fillets, fresh or frozen | ¼ cup melted margarine or butter |
| 1 teaspoon salt | 2 cups cooked rice |
| ¼ teaspoon pepper | Newburg Sauce, see below |
| | Paprika |

Thaw fish if frozen. Skin fillets and cut into serving size portions. Sprinkle with salt and pepper. Roll each fillet into a turban and secure with a toothpick. Place turbans on end in a well-greased baking dish, 8 × 8 × 2 inches. Brush with melted margarine. Bake in a moderate oven, 350 degrees F., for 15 to 20 minutes or until fish flakes easily when tested with a fork. To serve, remove toothpicks from turbans and place on a bed of rice. Spoon Newburg Sauce over turbans. Garnish with paprika.

Makes 6 servings.

## Newburg Sauce

½ cup margarine or butter
¼ cup all-purpose flour
½ teaspoon salt
⅛ teaspoon cayenne pepper

3 cups half and half
6 egg yolks, beaten
⅓ cup sherry

In a saucepan melt margarine. Stir in flour, salt, and cayenne. Add half and half gradually and cook until thick and smooth, stirring constantly. Stir a little of the hot sauce into the egg yolks; add to remaining sauce, stirring constantly. Remove from heat and slowly stir in sherry.

Makes approximately 4 cups.

## Super Grouper

2 pounds grouper fillets or other
    fish fillets, fresh or frozen
¼ cup chopped onion
1 package (⅝ to ⅞ ounces) brown
    gravy mix
1 tablespoon olive oil

1 teaspoon lemon juice
1 teaspoon salt
Dash pepper
¼ cup sliced almonds
¼ cup chopped green pepper

Thaw frozen fillets. Skin fillets. Cut fillets into serving size portions. Sprinkle onion in a well-greased baking dish, 13 × 9 × 2 inches. Place fish in a single layer on onion. Prepare brown gravy mix according to package directions. To gravy mix, add oil, lemon juice, salt, and pepper. Pour gravy mixture over fish. Bake in a moderate oven, 350 degrees F., for 20 to 25 minutes or until fish flakes easily when tested with a fork. Garnish with almonds and green pepper.

Makes 6 servings.

## Special Day Pollock

*Many of the settlers came to America seeking religious freedom. Two such groups were the the Amish and Mennonites who settled in Pennsylvania at the invitation of William Penn. Living far from the coast on scattered farms made it difficult for them to obtain the foods necessary for favorite European recipes. This was especially true of seafood. On those occasions that fish was available it was a special day.*

2 pounds pollock fillets or other
    fish fillets, fresh or frozen
2 quarts water
½ cup sliced onion
½ cup sliced carrot
1 stalk of celery, quartered

2 tablespoons lemon juice
1 tablespoon salt
8 peppercorns
Sour Sauce, see below
Salad greens

Thaw fillets if frozen. Divide into serving size portions. In a large skillet combine water, onion, carrots, celery, lemon juice, salt, and peppercorns. Bring to a boil; simmer for 10 minutes to blend flavors. Add fillets. Cover and simmer for 5 to 10 minutes or until fish flakes easily when tested with a fork. Carefully remove fish to a well-greased baking dish, 12 × 8 × 2 inches. Cook poaching liquid until it is reduced to 1½ cups; strain and reserve for Sour Sauce. Pour Sour Sauce over fish. Cover and chill for several hours, or overnight in the refrigerator. Serve on salad greens.

Makes 6 servings.

## Sour Sauce for Special Day Pollock

1½ cups poaching liquid
¼ cup chopped dill pickle
2 hard-cooked eggs, chopped
¼ cup tarragon vinegar
¼ cup olive oil

2 tablespoons capers, drained
1 tablespoon chopped parsley
⅛ teaspoon liquid hot pepper
    sauce
½ teaspoon salt

Combine poaching liquid, dill pickle, chopped eggs, vinegar, oil, capers, parsley, liquid hot pepper sauce, and salt.

Makes 2½ cups.

## Pollock Barbecue

*Early barbecues consisted of little more than a frame holding roasting meat. The Spanish settlers in the New World had a word for this—barbacoa. In time the concept of the barbecue expanded to include sauce, salads, side dishes, and desserts along with the main dish.*

1 pound pollock fillets or other fish fillets, fresh or frozen
½ cup barbecue sauce
1 can (1 pound) kidney beans, heated

4 hamburger rolls or French rolls, heated
½ cup fresh onion rings

Thaw fish if frozen. Cut into 4 servings. Place in a shallow dish. Pour barbecue sauce over fish and let marinate in the refrigerator for 1 hour, turning once or twice during the marinating process. Remove from marinade and place on a well-greased broiler pan. Broil about 4 inches from source of heat for 4 to 5 minutes. Turn fish and cook for 4 to 5 minutes longer or until fish flakes easily when tested with a fork. Place fish on bottom half of bun. Place kidney beans and onion rings on top of fish. Cover with top half of roll.

Makes 4 servings.

*Note:* Fish may be cooked over hot coals. Sandwiches may also be served open faced.

## Salmoncado Buns

1 can (7¾ ounces) salmon
1 small avocado, diced
½ cup chopped tomato
4 hamburger buns
2 tablespoons chopped onion

⅓ cup mayonnaise or salad dressing
Salt and pepper to taste
4 cherry tomatoes
Watercress

Drain and flake salmon. Combine with avocado, tomato, onion, mayonnaise, salt, and pepper. Spread on bottom half of hamburger buns. Garnish with cherry tomato and watercress.

Makes 4 sandwiches.

# Salmon Loaf

1 can (15 ounces) salmon
½ cup salad dressing
1 can (10½ ounces) cream of celery
    soup
1 egg, beaten
1 cup dry bread crumbs

½ cup chopped onion
¼ cup chopped green pepper
1 tablespoon lemon juice
1 teaspoon salt
Cucumber Sauce, see below

Combine salmon, drained and flaked, with salad dressing, cream of celery soup, beaten egg, bread crumbs, onion, green pepper, lemon juice, and salt. Pour into greased 8½ × 4½ inch loaf pan. Bake at 350 degrees F. for 1 hour. Serve with Cucumber Sauce.

Makes 8 servings.

# Cucumber Sauce

¼ cup mayonnaise or salad
    dressing

½ cup dairy sour cream
¼ cup chopped cucumber

Mix all ingredients and let stand for 1 hour to blend flavors.

Makes about 1 cup.

# Quick Deep Dish Salmon Pie

2 cans (10½ ounces each) pea or
    cream of asparagus soup
1 can (16 ounces or two 7¾
    ounces) salmon
½ cup milk or cream
⅛ teaspoon white pepper
¼ teaspoon oregano
¼ teaspoon sweet basil

1 can (16 ounces) small potatoes,
    drained
1 can (16 ounces) small onions,
    drained
1 package (8 ounces) refrigerator
    buttermilk biscuits
Watercress

In a saucepan combine soup, liquid from can of salmon, and the milk or cream. Stir in salmon, seasonings, potatoes, and onions. Heat until sauce begins to simmer, stirring occasionally. Empty into a

2-quart casserole, top with biscuits, and place in oven, 375 degrees F., for 15 to 20 minutes, or until biscuits are brown. Garnish with watercress.

Makes 4 to 6 servings.

## Salmon-Cheese Pie

2 cups all-purpose flour
3 teaspoons baking powder
½ teaspoon salt
⅓ cup shortening
2 unbeaten eggs
⅓ cup milk

1 can (16 ounces) salmon
1 tablespoon grated onion
⅓ pound thinly sliced American cheese
Vegetable Sauce, see below

Sift together flour, baking powder, and salt. Cut in shortening until particles are fine. Combine unbeaten eggs and milk; beat well. Add all at once to dry ingredients. Mix only until all particles are moistened. Roll out two-thirds of dough on floured surface until you have an 11-inch circle. Fit into 9-inch pie pan or layer cake pan. Drain salmon, reserving 2 tablespoons of the liquid. Flake into bowl; remove skin and bones. Add onion and the reserved salmon liquid. Turn into the pastry-lined pan. Cover with cheese. Roll out remaining dough to a 7-inch circle. Place on top of the cheese. Bake in moderate oven, 375 degrees F., for 25 to 30 minutes. Serve hot with Vegetable Sauce. Garnish with parsley if desired.

Makes 6 servings.

## Vegetable Sauce

¼ cup butter or margarine
¼ cup all-purpose flour
1 teaspoon prepared mustard

2 cups milk
½ teaspoon salt
2 cups cooked green vegetables

Melt butter or margarine in a saucepan. Blend in flour and mustard; mix well. Gradually add milk. Cook over low heat, stirring constantly, until thick. Add salt and green vegetables.

Makes about 4 cups.

## Salmon Supper Pie

1 can (15½ ounces or 439 grams) salmon
1 package (10 ounces) frozen broccoli spears, defrosted
¼ cup finely chopped onion
2 tablespoons margarine
2 tablespoons all-purpose flour
¾ cup milk
1 can (10¾ ounces) cream of celery soup
1 tablespoon lemon juice
½ teaspoon Worcestershire sauce
2 hard-cooked eggs, diced
2 tablespoons minced parsley
Cheese Pastry, see below

Drain salmon, reserving liquid. Separate salmon into chunks with a fork. Cut broccoli into large pieces. Saute onion in margarine. Blend in flour. Add reserved salmon liquid, milk, and soup. Cook, stirring constantly, until thickened and smooth. Blend in lemon juice, Worcestershire sauce, eggs, and parsley. Line a 9-inch pie plate with Cheese Pastry, leaving a 1-inch overhang. Arrange half of the salmon and broccoli in pie shell. Cover with half of the sauce. Repeat. Roll out remaining pastry and cut in ½-inch strips. Place strips of pastry over pie to form lattice. Moisten ends with water and press firmly to rim to seal. Turn overhang of bottom crust over edges of lattice strips and flute. Bake in hot oven, 400 degrees F., for 40 to 45 minutes.

Makes 6 servings.

## Cheese Pastry

1⅔ cups all-purpose flour
½ teaspoon salt
⅛ teaspoon cayenne pepper
1 cup grated sharp Cheddar cheese
6 tablespoons cooking oil
3 tablespoons ice water

Combine flour, salt, and pepper. Add Cheddar cheese, mixing thoroughly. Blend in oil. Add ice water, a tablespoon at a time, mixing until dough holds together.

Makes enough pastry for lattice-top 9-inch pie.

## Quick Salmon Rice Casserole

1 can (7¾ ounces) salmon
3 cups cooked rice
1 tablespoon lemon juice
¼ cup chopped celery
½ teaspoon dillweed

¾ cup shredded medium Cheddar
   cheese
1 can (10½ ounces) cream of
   mushroom soup
¼ cup milk

Flake salmon into buttered 1½-quart casserole. Mix in remaining ingredients. Bake at 350 degrees F. for 25 to 30 minutes.

Makes 4 servings.

## Salmon Scandia

*Salmon was one of the principal foods of the Indians along the northwest coast. Even as settlers with their different cooking traditions arrived from Scandinavia, Germany, and Russia, salmon continued to be important to the local food economy. This importance is reflected today in the various recipes for salmon.*

2 pounds salmon fillets or other
   fish fillets, fresh or frozen
1 tablespoon salt
3 cups water
1 cup vinegar
½ cup sugar

½ cup seedless raisins
6 thin lemon slices
1 bay leaf
1-inch stick cinnamon
12 gingersnaps, crushed coarsely
1 cup water

Thaw fish if frozen. Cut fish into 1-inch pieces. Dredge fish with salt; cover and chill for 1 hour. Combine 3 cups of water, vinegar, sugar, raisins, lemon slices, bay leaf, and cinnamon. Bring to a brisk boil. Rinse the salt from the fish and place fish in boiling liquid. Reduce heat and simmer for 5 to 7 minutes or until fish flakes easily when tested with a fork. Meanwhile, soak gingersnaps in 1 cup of water; add mixture to the fish. Simmer 1 minute longer. Serve hot or cold as a main dish or appetizer.

Makes 4 servings.

## Salmon Romanoff, St. George

*Russian sailors and fur-traders explored much of northwestern America throughout the eighteenth and nineteenth centuries. The largest of the Pribilof Islands, St. George, was named after Gerasim Pribilof's ship, the* St. George, *almost two hundred years ago. This early Russian influence can still be found in West Coast cuisine, particularly in the use of sour cream and caviar which are common ingredients in Russian cooking.*

1 can (7¾ ounces) salmon
1 package (6 ounces) egg noodles
    with Cheddar cheese and
    sour cream sauce
1 cup cream style cottage cheese

1 can (4 ounces) sliced mush-
    rooms, drained
3 tablespoons chopped green
    onion
¼ teaspoon dillweed

Flake salmon. Prepare noodles according to package directions. Combine prepared noodles with salmon, cottage cheese, mushrooms, green onion, and dill. Spoon into buttered 1½ quart casserole. Bake in a moderate oven, 350 degrees F., for 20 to 25 minutes.

Makes 4 servings.

## Salmon in Cheese

¼ cup butter or margarine
¼ cup all-purpose flour
½ teaspoon salt
½ teaspoon prepared mustard

2 cups milk
1 cup (¼ pound) shredded cheese
1 can (1 pound) salmon
½ cup cooked green vegetables

Melt butter in saucepan; blend in flour, salt, and mustard. Gradually stir in milk. Cook, stirring constantly, until thick. Add cheese; stir until melted. Stir in drained, flaked salmon and vegetables. Heat thoroughly.

Makes 4 servings.

## Salmon Piquante

1½ to 2 pounds salmon fillets,
    skin on
Salt
1 medium onion, sliced
1 lemon, sliced

1 teaspoon mixed pickling spice
1 clove garlic, finely chopped
½ cup mayonnaise or salad
    dressing
1 cucumber, sliced

Salt salmon. Arrange onion, lemon, spice, and garlic in a well-greased casserole. Place salmon, skin side up, over seasonings. Cover tightly and bake in a moderate oven, 350 degrees F., for one hour. Chill salmon in covered casserole. (If your casserole does not have a cover, use aluminum foil over top for an improvised cover.) Place on a serving platter and remove skins carefully. Garnish with mayonnaise and cucumber.

Makes 6 servings.

## Potlatch Salmon

*Many Indian tribes of the Pacific Northwest celebrated special events with a great feast that might last for several days. The potlatch, as such feasts were known, included an enormous amount of seafood, particularly salmon, and provided an opportunity for families to display their social rank. Frequently the hosts gave away furs and other goods.*

2 pounds salmon steaks or other
    fish steaks, fresh or frozen (6
    steaks)
1 tablespoon juniper berries (about
    50)

¼ cup salad oil
2 teaspoons salt
⅛ teaspoon pepper
Lemon or lime wedges
Mayonnaise

Thaw fish if frozen. Lightly crush juniper berries. Push 6 to 8 berries into each steak. Coat fish with oil to prevent sticking. Sprinkle fish with salt and pepper. Grill over hot coals 5 to 6 minutes on each side. Fish may be broiled or panfried for approximately the same length of time. Garnish with lemon wedges and mayonnaise.

Makes 6 servings.

## Twice-Canned Salmon

*The flesh of the salmon is remarkably compact and tasty. This is one of the reasons for the great popularity of the fish over the years. The first salmon cannery was started by William Hume and Andrew Hopgood on the Sacramento River in 1864. Two years later they moved their cannery north to the Columbia River. Along with salmon, the following recipe takes advantage of apples, another well-known food of the Pacific Northwest.*

1 can (16 ounces) salmon
1¼ cups grated unpeeled apples
1 cup fresh bread crumbs (2 slices bread)
½ cup milk
2 eggs, beaten
⅓ cup chopped parsley

2 tablespoons instant minced onion
¼ teaspoon salt
⅛ teaspoon pepper
Parsley sprigs
Lemon wedges

Drain salmon and reserve liquid; flake. Combine salmon and liquid with remaining ingredients except parsley sprigs and lemon wedges. Place salmon in a well-greased one-pound coffee can. Cover can with a double thickness of aluminum foil and secure with string or a heavy wire twist. Place can in a pot of boiling water; water should reach to two-thirds the depth of the can. Cover and simmer for one hour. Remove can from water and allow to cool for 5 to 10 minutes before unmolding salmon loaf. Remove foil cover and run a spatula or thin knife around edge of loaf to loosen. Unmold onto serving platter. Garnish with parsley sprigs and lemon wedges. Loaf is excellent cold, sliced, and served with slices of raw onion.

Makes 6 servings.

## Salmon Pudding—Norwegian Style

1½ pounds salmon
2 teaspoons salt
¼ teaspoon nutmeg

¼ cup butter or other fat, melted
2 cups milk

Remove skin and bones from salmon; grind enough to make 2 cups. Place fish, salt, and nutmeg in large bowl and beat 10 minutes with an electric beater. Add butter slowly and continue beating. Add milk, ½ cup at a time, beating after each addition. Beat 15 minutes after final addition and place in a well-greased casserole. Place in a pan of hot water and bake in a moderate oven, 350 degrees F., for 1½ hours or until it tests done as for custard. Serve hot.

Makes 4 to 6 servings.

## Salmon Pie—Russian Style

1 can (1 pound) salmon
¼ cup salmon liquor
1 cup cooked rice
1 tablespoon lemon juice
1 medium onion, grated

2 stalks celery, chopped
2 tablespoons butter or other fat
2 cups pastry mix, or 2 cups pre-
    pared mashed potatoes

Drain and flake salmon. Combine salmon, liquor, rice, lemon juice, onion, and celery. Prepare 1 cup mashed potato or 1 cup pastry; and place half in casserole dish leaving cavity for fish. Place fish mixture in casserole and dot with butter. Cover casserole with remaining pastry or mashed potatoes and score top. Bake in a hot oven, 400 degrees F., 45 minutes or until brown.

Makes 4 servings.

## Salmon Casserole Surprise

1 can (1 pound) salmon
3 tablespoons butter or other fat
3 tablespoons all-purpose flour
Salmon liquor and enough milk to
    make 2 cups
4 cups sliced cooked potatoes

½ cup mayonnaise or salad
    dressing
½ cup grated cheese
1 teaspoon Worcestershire sauce
1 teaspoon prepared mustard

Drain and flake salmon, reserving liquor. Melt fat; blend in flour. Add liquid gradually; cook until thick and smooth, stirring constantly. Arrange potatoes, salmon, and sauce in alternate layers in a well-greased casserole. Mix mayonnaise, cheese, mustard, and Worcestershire sauce; spread over top of fish mixture. Bake in a moderate oven, 375 degrees F., 30 minutes.

Makes 6 servings.

## Door County Fish Boil

*Door County is a peninsula in Wisconsin that extends out into Lake Michigan. It is thought that the fish boil originated as a summer activity to enjoy the cool breezes of the lake. Fish, vegetables, and sauce were cooked in huge iron kettles over outdoor fires. The following recipe recaptures much of the spirit of those early fish boils.*

2 pounds whitefish or other fish
     fillets, fresh or frozen
10 cups water
⅓ cup salt
12 small red potatoes
6 medium onions, peeled

6 wedges cabbage
1 can (1 pound) small whole beets
Horseradish Sauce, see Sauces
     chapter
Chopped parsley

Thaw fish if frozen. Cut into serving size portions. In a large pot heat water and salt to boiling. Remove a ½-inch strip of peeling around middle of potatoes. Add potatoes and onion to water; simmer 30 minutes or until fork tender. Add cabbage wedges; simmer about 10 minutes until tender. Add fish and simmer 3 to 4 minutes or until fish flakes easily when tested with a fork. Remove vegetables and fish to a serving platter and keep warm. Add beets to water and heat. Remove beets to platter with other vegetables and fish. Pour Horse-radish Sauce over vegetables and fish. Garnish with finely chopped parsley.

Makes 6 servings.

## Butterfish in Spanish Sauce

*California cooking has been influenced by many traditions. When the Spanish explored and settled Mexico, they introduced the to-mato which Mexican cooks combined with native ingredients to make what was a new, tasty sauce. As the Spanish moved north-ward into California, they brought this prized sauce with them.*

1½ pounds Pacific butterfish fil-
　　lets or other fish fillets,
　　fresh or frozen
2 tablespoons margarine or butter
1 cup chopped onion

½ cup chopped green pepper
1 can (1 pound) tomatoes, un-
　　drained, cut up
1 teaspoon salt
⅛ teaspoon pepper

Thaw fish if frozen. Cut fish into 4 portions. In a saucepan melt margarine. Add onion and green pepper; cook until tender. Add tomatoes, salt, and pepper. Cover and simmer for 8 to 10 minutes. Add fish. Spoon sauce over fish; cover and cook for 8 to 10 minutes or until fish flakes easily when tested with a fork.

Makes 4 servings.

## Boston Bean Skillet

1½ pounds ocean perch fillets or
　　other fish fillets, fresh or
　　frozen
1 teaspoon salt
¼ teaspoon pepper
4 slices bacon, diced
1 cup chopped onion
1 clove garlic, crushed

½ cup light brown sugar
2 tablespoons prepared mustard
1 can (1 pound) lima beans,
　　undrained
1 can (1 pound) butter beans with
　　molasses and bacon,
　　undrained

Thaw fish if frozen. Cut into serving size portions. Sprinkle with salt and pepper. In a large skillet cook bacon until almost done. Add onion and garlic and cook until onion is tender. Stir in brown sugar, mustard, lima beans, and butter beans. Bring mixture to a boil and simmer for 20 to 25 minutes, stirring occasionally. Place fillets on top of beans in skillet in a single layer. Cover and simmer for 4 to 5 minutes or until fish flakes easily when tested with a fork.

Makes 6 servings.

# Sanddabs, Grant Avenue

*Sanddabs are found only in Western waters. They are the smallest members of the sole family, and have a distinctive flavor that lends itself easily to various recipes. Sanddabs, Grant Avenue, which draws on the subtle influences of Chinese cooking, is one of the most delicious ways of preparing these delicate fish.*

| | |
|---|---|
| 3 pounds dressed sanddabs or other dressed fish, fresh or frozen | 4 whole green onions |
| | 1 quart boiling water |
| | ⅓ cup salad oil, heated |
| 1 tablespoon peeled, grated ginger root | ⅓ cup soy sauce |
| | Green onions |
| 2 teaspoons salt | |

Thaw fish if frozen. Clean, wash, and dry fish. Arrange fish on heat-proof platter; sprinkle with ginger and salt. Place whole green onions on top of fish. Place platter on a trivet or rack inside a steamer or large roaster containing the boiling water. Cover and cook over boiling water for 5 to 10 minutes, or until fish flakes easily when tested with a fork. Remove fish from steamer. Discard cooked onions and drain any water from the platter. Combine oil and soy sauce and pour sauce over fish; garnish with green onions.

Makes 6 servings.

# Sheepshead with Drawn Butter

| | |
|---|---|
| 2 pounds sheepshead fillets or other fish fillets, fresh or frozen | 1 cup margarine or butter |
| | ¼ cup all-purpose flour |
| | ¼ cup lemon juice |
| 1 teaspoon salt | 2 tablespoons chopped parsley |
| ¼ teaspoon pepper | |

Thaw fillets if frozen. Sprinkle fillets with salt and pepper. Place fish in a well-greased steamer insert pan. Cover and steam over boiling water for 5 to 10 minutes or until fish flakes easily when tested with a fork. Cut margarine into eight pieces; roll into balls, then in flour to coat. Put two balls of margarine in a small saucepan. Melt margarine and stir with a wire whisk until smooth. Add remaining margarine and whisk until melted and smooth. Stir in lemon juice and parsley. Heat just until flour is cooked. Serve drawn butter in a sauceboat with fish.

Makes 6 servings.

## Whiting, Gloucester Style

*Whiting ranges from the Mediterranean to Iceland and the eastern coast of America. It likes shallow waters and is easily caught close to shore. The European settlers were familiar with whiting, known by various names throughout Europe, and quickly adapted its cooking to the New World.*

2 pounds whiting fillets or other fish fillets, fresh or frozen
½ teaspoon salt
½ teaspoon garlic salt
¼ teaspoon pepper
1 cup all-purpose flour
¼ cup margarine or butter
¼ cup cooking oil
2 tablespoons margarine or butter

¼ cup chopped onion
2 tablespoons chopped green pepper
1 clove garlic, crushed
1 can (1 pound) tomatoes, undrained, cut up
¼ teaspoon leaf thyme
3 slices (1 ounce each) cheese, cut in half

Thaw fish if frozen. Divide into serving size portions. Sprinkle with salt, garlic salt, and pepper. Roll fish in flour. Heat ¼ cup margarine and ¼ cup cooking oil in frying pan until hot, but not smoking. Place fish in pan and fry at a moderate heat for 4 to 5 minutes until browned. Turn carefully and fry for 4 to 5 minutes longer or until fish is browned and flakes easily when tested with a fork. In a saucepan melt 2 tablespoons margarine. Add onion, green pepper, and garlic and cook until tender. Add tomatoes and thyme. Heat sauce. Pour sauce into a baking dish, 12 × 8 × 2 inches. Place fish on top of sauce. Arrange cheese on top of fish. Bake fish in a moderate oven, 350 degrees F., for 8 to 10 minutes or until cheese melts.

Makes 6 servings.

# Svenskie Smelt Fry

*When the Scandinavians came to America they looked to settle on lands that were similar to the ones they left. The colder climate of the northern territories reminded them of home. Like other settlers the Scandinavians brought along traditional recipes, adapting them to local ingredients. The following recipe, combining the delicate taste of smelt with anchovy, has a distinctive Swedish flavor.*

20 medium smelt or other small
    fish, fresh or frozen (about 1
    pound)
1 can (2 ounces) anchovy fillets
¼ teaspoon salt
⅛ teaspoon pepper
½ cup all-purpose flour
3 tablespoons margarine or butter

3 tablespoons cooking oil
4 slices rye bread, crusts removed,
    toasted
Svenskie Sauce, see below
Sliced tomatoes and cucumber,
    optional
Lemon twists and dill sprigs for
    garnish

Thaw fish if frozen. Remove heads from fish, clean, and bone. Drain anchovies, reserving oil for Svenskie Sauce. Cut anchovies in half lengthwise. Place one half anchovy inside each fish. Sprinkle fish with salt and pepper. Roll in flour. In large skillet heat margarine and cooking oil to a moderate temperature. Add fish and fry until crisp. Place 5 fish on each slice of rye toast. Spoon Svenskie Sauce over smelt. Serve with sliced tomatoes and cucumber.
Garnish with lemon twists and dill sprigs.

Makes 4 servings.

# Svenskie Sauce

Reserved anchovy oil from previ-
    ous recipe
2 tablespoons minced onion
1½ tablespoons all-purpose flour
½ teaspoon salt

1⅓ cups half and half
1 egg yolk, beaten
1 tablespoon lemon juice
1 tablespoon chopped fresh dill (or
    ½ teaspoon dried dillweed)

In a saucepan cook onion in anchovy oil until tender. Blend in flour and salt. Gradually stir in half and half. Cook until thickened, stirring constantly. Add a little of the hot sauce to the egg yolk; add to remaining sauce, stirring constantly. Heat until thickened. Add lemon juice and dill.

Makes 1⅓ cups.

# Winnibigoshish Walleye and Wild Rice

*Walleyed pike, abundant in the Upper Great Lakes region, was an important food to the Indians in the area. Wild rice was also popular with the Indians. It was only a matter of time before the two would be combined to form the basis of a unique dish.*

2 pounds walleyed pike fillets or
    other fish fillets, fresh or
    frozen
1 teaspoon salt
¼ teaspoon pepper
3 slices bacon, diced
1 cup chopped fresh mushrooms
    (about ¼ pound)

¼ cup minced onion
¼ cup minced celery
2 cups cooked wild rice
½ teaspoon salt
2 tablespoons melted margarine or
    butter
Mushroom-Walnut Sauce, see
    Sauces chapter

Thaw fillets if frozen. Cut fillets into serving size portions. Season fillets with 1 teaspoon salt and ¼ teaspoon pepper. In a skillet, cook bacon until lightly browned. Add mushrooms, onion, and celery; cook until tender. Stir in cooked rice and salt. Place pike fillets in a well-greased baking pan. Place approximately ½ cup rice mixture on top of each fillet. Drizzle the 2 tablespoons melted margarine over rice. Cover. Bake in a moderate oven, 350 degrees F., for about 20 minutes or until fish flakes easily when tested with a fork. Serve with Mushroom-Walnut Sauce.

Makes 4 to 6 servings.

# Connecticut Planked Shad

*When the Dutch first arrived in the New World, they learned from the Indians how to bake fish on shingles. It wasn't long before the Dutch adapted this method to cook shad over a fire on a fish plank.*

3- to 4-pound shad, split and
    boned, or other dressed fish,
    fresh or frozen
2 teaspoons salt

⅛ teaspoon pepper
¼ cup melted margarine or butter
Soufflé, see below

Thaw fish if frozen. Sprinkle inside and outside with salt and pepper. Place fish, skin side down, on a well-greased plank or baking tray, 18 × 13 × 1 inches. Brush with melted margarine. Bake in a moderate oven, 350 degrees F., for 40 to 60 minutes or until fish flakes easily when tested with a fork. Spread soufflé over fish. Return to the oven and bake for 10 to 15 minutes longer or until soufflé is done and browned.

Makes 6 servings.

# Soufflé

¼ cup margarine or butter
¼ cup minced onion
½ cup all-purpose flour
½ teaspoon salt
1 cup milk
¼ cup white wine

1 tablespoon lemon juice
3 egg yolks, beaten
½ cup chopped parsley
3 egg whites, beaten until stiff
1 jar (3½ ounces) caviar, optional*

In a saucepan, melt margarine. Add onion and cook until tender. Blend in flour and salt. Gradually stir in milk, wine, and lemon juice. Cook until thickened, stirring constantly. Blend a little of the hot sauce into the egg yolks; add to remaining sauce, stirring constantly. Heat just until mixture thickens. Stir in chopped parsley. Fold in egg whites and caviar. Bake in a greased 7-inch soufflé baker until firm, about 40 minutes, at 350 degrees F.

Makes 4 servings.

*If fresh shad roe is available, cook it in salted vinegar water. Remove membrane and use in place of caviar.

## Fisherman Potatoes au Gratin

2 cans (3¾ or 4 ounces each)
   sardines
2 tablespoons chopped onion
2 tablespoons melted fat or oil
2 tablespoons all-purpose flour
1 teaspoon salt
Dash pepper
2 cups milk

1 cup shredded cheese
2 teaspoons Worcestershire sauce
5 cups sliced, cooked potatoes
¾ cup soft bread cubes
2 tablespoons butter or margarine,
   melted
Paprika

Drain sardines. Cook onion in fat until tender. Blend in flour and seasonings. Add milk gradually and cook until thickened, stirring constantly. Add cheese and Worcestershire sauce. Stir until cheese melts. Arrange half the potatoes in a well-greased, 1½-quart casserole. Cover with sardines and remaining potatoes. Pour sauce over potatoes. Toss bread cubes with butter and sprinkle over top of casserole. Sprinkle with paprika. Bake in a moderate oven, 350 degrees F., for 25 to 30 minutes or until lightly browned.

Makes 6 servings.

## Penobscot Bay Fish Pudding

2 cans (3¾ or 4 ounces each)
   sardines
4 cups sliced, cooked potatoes
½ teaspoon salt
⅛ teaspoon pepper
2 tablespoons minced onion

1½ cups half and half
2 eggs, beaten
1 tablespoon all-purpose flour
½ cup shredded Cheddar cheese
Tomatoes, sliced thin

Drain sardines. Cut sardines in half lengthwise. Place a layer of sliced potatoes in a well-greased 1½-quart round casserole. Arrange sardines over potatoes. Top with remaining potatoes. Combine half and half, eggs, flour, salt, and pepper. Pour over potatoes and sardines. Bake in a moderate oven, 350 degrees F., for 35 to 40 minutes or until knife inserted near center comes out clean. Sprinkle casserole with cheese; return casserole to oven just until cheese melts. Garnish with thin tomato slices.

Makes 6 servings.

## Pompano en Papillote

*Throughout history special dishes have been created for special occasions. Antoine's of New Orleans honored Brazilian balloonist Alberto Santos-Dumont during his visit to the city in 1901 with a dish designed like a flying balloon. The fish, which was covered by rich shrimp sauce, was baked inside a closed envelope of baking parchment. The creation was considered one of Antoine's most famous.*

2 pounds pompano fillets or other fish fillets, fresh or frozen
1 can (6½ or 7 ounces) crabmeat, drained, flaked, and cartilage removed
¼ pound cooked, peeled, and deveined shrimp, fresh or frozen
3 cups water
1 teaspoon salt
2 lemon slices
1 bay leaf

⅛ teaspoon dried thyme leaves, crushed
Parchment or brown paper
2 tablespoons cooking oil
½ cup chopped green onion
1 clove garlic, minced
2 tablespoons margarine or butter
3 tablespoons all-purpose flour
¼ teaspoon salt
2 egg yolks, slightly beaten
3 tablespoons dry white wine

Thaw fish if frozen. Chop shrimp. In 10-inch fry pan bring water, 1 teaspoon salt, lemon, bay leaf, and thyme to a boil. Add fish, cover, and simmer for about 10 minutes or until fish flakes easily when tested with a fork. Carefully remove fish. Strain stock, reserving 1½ cups. Remove skin and bones from fish. Cut 6 pieces parchment or brown paper into heart shapes about 10 × 12 inches each. Brush paper with oil. Place one fillet on half of each paper heart. In saucepan melt margarine. Add onion and garlic and cook until tender. Blend in flour and ¼ teaspoon salt. Add reserved stock. Cook, stirring constantly, until thickened. Gradually stir small amount of hot mixture into egg yolks; add to remaining sauce, stirring constantly. Heat just until mixture thickens. Stir in wine, crabmeat, and shrimp. Heat. Spoon about ½ cup sauce over each fillet. Fold other half of each paper heart over fillet to form individual cases. Seal, starting at top of heart, by turning edges up and folding, twisting tip of heart to hold case closed. Place cases in shallow baking pan. Bake in a hot oven, 400 degrees F., for 10 to 15 minutes. To serve, cut cases open with large X design on top; fold back each segment.

Makes 6 servings.

## Planked Maine Sardines

4 cans (3¾ or 4 ounces each)
    sardines
1 can (4 ounces) sliced mush-
    rooms, drained
2 tablespoons butter or margarine,
    melted
3 cups seasoned mashed potatoes

1 can (1 pound) whole carrots,
    drained
1 can (1 pound) whole onions,
    drained
¼ cup butter or margarine, melted
¼ cup chopped parsley

Drain sardines. Place in the center of a well-greased bake-and-serve platter, 16 × 10 inches. Combine mushrooms and butter. Spread over sardines. Arrange a border of mashed potatoes around sardines. Combine carrots, onions, butter, and parsley. Arrange carrots and onions around sardines. Bake in a moderate oven, 350 degrees F., for 20 to 25 minutes or until heated.

Makes 6 to 8 servings.

## Fish Steaks Baked-in-the-Coals

2 pounds fish steaks, fillets, or
    a whole trout*
Salt and pepper

¼ cup butter, melted
6 onion slices
6 lemon slices

Cut fish in serving size portions. Sprinkle with salt and pepper. Brush both sides with melted butter. Divide the ingredients into 6 portions. Place an onion slice and a lemon slice on top of each portion. Wrap each portion in aluminum foil; seal well. Place on a bed of hot coals and cook 10 minutes, turning frequently for even cooking. Serve while hot directly from the foil package.

Makes 6 servings.

*To bake a whole fish: Proceed as for steaks. Cover fish with bacon strips. Increase baking time to ½ hour for 3- to 4-pound fish.

## Black Drum with Zesty Sauce

*The black drum, also known as the sea drum, is abundant from the Carolinas southward, although it can be found as far north as New York. It produces a humming sound by repeated contraction of a specialized muscle. Combined with sauce and seasonings black drum is an uncommon dish.*

2 pounds black drum or other fish
   fillets, fresh or frozen
½ cup catsup
¼ cup salad oil
¼ cup lemon juice

1 tablespoon grated onion
1 teaspoon Worcestershire sauce
1 teaspoon prepared mustard
½ teaspoon garlic salt
¼ teaspoon salt

Thaw fish if frozen. Combine remaining ingredients in shallow bowl. Add fillets, turning to moisten both sides with sauce. Cover and place in refrigerator to marinate 1 hour. Remove fish from marinade and reserve sauce for basting. Place fish in a single layer on a foil-lined baking pan, 15 × 10 × 1 inches. Broil about 4 inches from source of heat for 10 to 15 minutes or until fish flakes easily when tested with a fork. Baste once during broiling with remaining sauce. Fish need not be turned during broiling.

Makes 6 servings.

# Main Dishes—
## Shellfish, Crabs, Squid, Etc.

# Creole Jambalaya

*Based on French and Spanish cooking, Creole Jambalaya is considered one of the classic Creole dishes. It can be made with shellfish, poultry, and ham, either together or separately. A variety of other ingredients, which also are included at the chef's discretion, makes this dish unique with each serving.*

1½ pounds raw, peeled, and deveined shrimp, fresh or frozen
2 tablespoons margarine or butter
¾ cup chopped onion
½ cup chopped celery
¼ cup chopped green pepper
1 tablespoon chopped parsley
1 clove garlic, minced
1 can (28 ounces) tomatoes, undrained, cut up

2 cups cubed, fully cooked ham
1 can (10½ ounces) beef broth plus 1 can water
1 cup uncooked long grain rice
1 teaspoon sugar
½ teaspoon dried thyme leaves, crushed
½ teaspoon chili powder
¼ teaspoon pepper

Thaw shrimp if frozen. Melt margarine in Dutch oven. Add onion, celery, green pepper, parsley, and garlic. Cover and cook until tender. Add remaining ingredients, except shrimp. Cover and simmer 25 minutes or until rice is tender. Add shrimp. Simmer uncovered to desired consistency and until shrimp are cooked, about 5 to 10 minutes.

Makes 6 to 8 servings.

## Lobster House Special

3 live lobsters (about 1¾ pounds each)
⅓ cup margarine or butter
1½ cups chopped fresh mushrooms
3 tablespoons minced onion
1½ tablespoons all-purpose flour
¼ teaspoon liquid hot pepper sauce
¾ teaspoon salt
1½ cups half and half
3 egg yolks, beaten
3 tablespoons brandy
2 tablespoons chopped parsley
3 tablespoons fresh bread crumbs
3 tablespoons grated Parmesan cheese
½ teaspoon paprika
1 tablespoon melted margarine or butter

Place lobsters, head first, into a large pot of boiling water. Cover and simmer 15 to 20 minutes until lobsters are done. Legs will twist off easily when done. Remove lobster from pot. Cut off antennae. Twist off claws of lobster. Crack and remove meat. Using scissors cut through the soft stomach shell; remove the tail meat being careful to keep shells intact. Save the red coral roe, if any. Discard the stomach; set aside the shells. Cut the lobster meat into ½-inch cubes and set aside. In a skillet melt margarine. Add mushrooms and onion and cook until tender. Stir in flour, liquid hot pepper sauce, and salt. Gradually blend in half and half. Cook, stirring constantly, until thick. Add a little hot sauce to egg yolks; add to remaining sauce, stirring constantly. Heat until thickened. Stir in brandy, parsley, reserved lobster meat, and red coral roe, if any. Divide lobster mixture into shells or ramekins. Place shells on a baking tray. Combine bread crumbs, Parmesan cheese, paprika, and margarine. Sprinkle crumb mixture over lobsters. Bake in a moderate oven, 350 degrees F., for 15 to 20 minutes or until hot.

Makes 6 servings.

## Boiled Lobster

*Since the 1930s lobster fisheries have expanded rapidly in response to the growing popularity of the shellfish. When boiling lobster one should remember that males are better than females for boiling, and that small or medium-sized lobsters are usually better eating than large ones.*

2 live lobsters (1 pound each) or 2 frozen whole green lobsters (1 pound each)
3 quarts boiling water
3 tablespoons salt
Clarified or drawn butter (the terms are interchangeable)

Thaw lobsters if frozen. In a 6-quart kettle, bring the water and salt to a rolling boil. Plunge the live lobsters head first (or place the thawed green lobsters) into the boiling, salted water. Cover and return to full boil. Reduce the heat and simmer for 12 to 15 minutes. (Larger lobster will require a little longer cooking time.) Drain and rinse with cold water for 1 to 2 minutes. Split and clean lobster. Serve with the clarified butter. Frozen spiny lobster tails can be cooked by the same method. Increase the salt to ½ cup for six spiny lobster tails (5 to 8 ounces each). Reduce the cooking time to 5 to 10 minutes, depending on the size. Drain and rinse in cold water for 1 minute. Cut in half lengthwise and serve with clarified butter.

Makes 2 servings.

## Batter Fried Shrimp

1½ pounds raw, peeled, deveined shrimp, fresh or frozen
½ cup cooking oil
1 egg, beaten
1 cup all-purpose flour
½ cup milk
¼ cup water
¾ teaspoon seasoned salt
¼ teaspoon salt
Fat for deep frying

Thaw shrimp if frozen. Combine cooking oil and egg; beat well. Add the remaining ingredients and stir until well blended. Dip each shrimp into the batter. Drop the shrimp into the hot deep fat, 350 degrees F., and fry for ½ to 1 minute or until golden brown. Remove with slotted spoon; drain on absorbent paper and serve immediately.

Makes 6 servings.

## Shrimp and Broccoli en Casserole

*There are several varieties of shrimp found in American waters, mostly from the Carolinas southwards. In several areas of the country shrimp are considered a delicacy, and are the basis for many excellent recipes.*

1 pound cooked, peeled, deveined shrimp, fresh or frozen
⅓ cup finely chopped onion
½ cup melted margarine or cooking oil
2 tablespoons chopped parsley
2 tablespoons lemon juice
¾ teaspoon tarragon leaves

½ teaspoon salt
2 packages (10 ounces each) frozen broccoli, chopped or spears, cooked and drained
¼ cup fine corn flake crumbs
¼ cup grated Parmesan cheese
Lemon or tomato wedges, for garnish

Thaw shrimp if frozen. Cut large shrimp in half. Cook onion in margarine until tender, but not brown. Add the shrimp and heat. Stir in parsley, lemon juice, tarragon, and salt. Place equal amounts of chopped broccoli or quartered broccoli spears into 6 well-greased, 10-ounce baking dishes or ramekins. Top each with an equal amount of shrimp mixture. Combine the crumbs and cheese; mix well. Sprinkle over the shrimp mixture. Bake in a moderate oven, 350 degrees F., for 12 to 15 minutes or until thoroughly heated. Garnish with lemon or tomato wedges.

Makes 6 servings.

## Jiffy Shrimp Jambalaya

1 can (4½ ounces) shrimp
3 tablespoons cooking oil
¾ cup (about ¼ pound) cubed lean ham
1 can (14½ ounces) stewed tomatoes

1¼ cups uncooked rice
1 bay leaf
¼ teaspoon thyme
1 garlic clove, sliced
Dash or two cayenne pepper
1½ cups water

Have shrimp chilled in the can. Do not drain. Heat oil in a heavy pan or Dutch oven and saute ham about 2 minutes. Add tomatoes (solid pieces chopped), rice, seasonings, and water. Cook rapidly, uncovered, 5 minutes and then turn heat to its lowest point. Add shrimp and any liquid in the can. Toss lightly with a fork to mix. Cover closely and steam without stirring for 15 minutes or until rice is tender and liquid is absorbed.

Makes 2 to 4 servings.

## Shrimp and Corn Pudding

1 can (4½ ounces) shrimp
½ cup chopped onion
2 tablespoons butter
2 tablespoons all-purpose flour
1½ cups milk
2 eggs, well beaten
1 teaspoon salt

¼ teaspoon cayenne pepper
2 teaspoons sugar
¼ teaspoon nutmeg
1 tablespoon minced fresh parsley
1 box (10 ounces) frozen whole
    kernel corn, or 2 cups canned
    corn, drained

Drain shrimp. Preheat oven to 350 degrees F. In a saucepan, saute onion in butter about 5 minutes; blend in flour and remove from heat. Add milk, eggs, seasonings, corn, and shrimp. Turn into a 1½-quart casserole. Set dish in a pan containing a little water. Bake 50 minutes or until pudding is firm and lightly browned.

Makes 4 servings.

## Shrimp Noodle Bake

1 pound fresh or frozen, peeled and
    deveined shrimp
1 package (8 ounces) medium egg
    noodles, cooked and drained
½ pint (1 cup) dairy sour cream
1 can (10¾ ounces) cream of
    mushroom soup

¼ cup sliced green onion with 2
    inches of green tops
¼ cup sliced, pitted ripe olives
1 teaspoon dillweed
½ teaspoon seasoned salt
1 cup shredded Cheddar cheese

Thaw shrimp if frozen. Cut shrimp in half lengthwise, if desired. Combine noodles, sour cream, soup, onion, olives, dillweed, seasoned salt, and half of the cheese; mix well. Fold in shrimp and spoon into a shallow 2-quart baking dish. Cover with aluminum foil, crimping it securely to edges of the dish. Bake in a preheated oven, 350 degrees F., for 30 minutes. Uncover; sprinkle with remaining cheese. Return to the oven for about 15 minutes or until cheese melts.

Makes 4 to 6 servings.

## Smoked Butterfly Shrimp

2 pounds unpeeled, fresh jumbo
  shrimp
1½ cups butter-flavored cooking
  oil

Seafood seasoning or seasoned salt
Tartar sauce*

Butterfly shrimp by using scissors or sharp knife to make a deep cut through the top shell without cutting completely through the flesh. Remove sand vein, rinse, and spread in butterfly fashion. Place the shrimp, shell side down, on the grill over low coals and wet hickory chips. Brush generously with oil and sprinkle with seasoning. Cook at a moderately low temperature, approximately 200 degrees F., for 15 minutes, basting once or twice with oil. Turn each shrimp and continue cooking 4 to 5 minutes longer. Serve with Tartar Sauce.

Makes 6 servings.

*A commercially prepared Tartar sauce may be used or try the recipe in the Sauces chapter. It has an exceptionally fine taste and after trying it you may never want to go back to a commercial preparation again.

## Pickled Shrimp

2 pounds raw Gulf shrimp, peeled
  and cleaned
2 medium onions, sliced into rings
1½ cups vegetable oil
1½ cups white vinegar

½ cup sugar
1½ teaspoons salt
1½ teaspoons celery seed
4 tablespoons capers with juice

Place thawed shrimp in boiling salted water for 3 to 5 minutes or until pink and tender. Drain and rinse with cold water, then chill. Make alternate layers of shrimp and onion rings in a sealable container. Mix the remaining ingredients and pour over the shrimp and onions. Seal and place in the refrigerator for 6 hours or more, shaking or inverting occasionally. Remove shrimp from marinade and serve.

Makes 4 servings.

*Serving suggestion:* This makes a nice light supper on a warm night. Serve the pickled shrimp on individual lettuce beds with green beans either tossed with dill, or buttered and tossed with grated Parmesan cheese, and a baked potato. Follow with a fruit and light cheese for dessert and you'll have a very special supper.

## Golden Fried Shrimp

1½ pounds raw Gulf shrimp, with shells on
2 eggs, beaten
1 teaspoon salt

½ cup all-purpose flour
½ cup dry bread crumbs or yellow cornmeal

Peel shrimp, leaving the last section of the shell on. Cut shrimp lengthwise along the back to expose the sand vein, then wash under cold running water. Combine eggs and salt. Mix together flour and crumbs. Dip each shrimp in the egg mixture and then roll in the flour and crumb mixture. Drop in hot oil, 375 degrees F., for 2 or 3 minutes or until golden brown. Drain on absorbent paper.

Makes 6 to 8 servings.

## Shrimp Supreme

3 pounds cleaned raw shrimp
2 cans (4 ounces each) sliced mushrooms, drained
⅔ cup butter or margarine, melted
½ cup chopped parsley
¼ cup chopped onion

2 tablespoons lemon juice
2 tablespoons chili sauce
1 teaspoon salt
½ teaspoon garlic salt
Dash Worcestershire sauce
Dash liquid hot pepper sauce

Cut six squares of heavy-duty aluminum foil, 12 inches each. Divide shrimp into six portions. Place each portion of shrimp on one half of each square of foil. Place mushrooms on top of shrimp. Combine remaining ingredients. Pour sauce over mushrooms, dividing evenly among portions. Fold other half of foil over shrimp and seal edges by making double folds in the foil. Place packages about 4 inches from moderately hot coals. Cook 10 to 12 minutes or until shrimp is tender. To serve, cut around edges and fold the foil back.

Makes 6 servings.

## Carolina Shrimp Pilau

*Rice was smuggled into South Carolina from Madagascar in 1680 by Captain John Thurber. The rice quickly flourished in the mild Carolina climate, becoming so important to the economy that by the eighteenth century it was used as a form of currency. Quite naturally it also became important to many Southern dishes.*

2 pounds raw, peeled, and deveined shrimp, fresh or frozen
8 slices bacon
2 cups chopped onion
1½ cups uncooked long grain rice
1 can (28 ounces) tomatoes, undrained, cut up

3 cups chicken broth or bouillon
2 teaspoons Worcestershire sauce
1 teaspoon salt
1 teaspoon ground mace
¼ teaspoon cayenne pepper
2 tablespoons chopped parsley

Thaw shrimp if frozen. In a heavy 3- to 4-quart Dutch oven cook bacon until crisp. Remove bacon. Drain on absorbent paper. Crumble and set aside. Reserve 3 tablespoons bacon fat. Add onion to reserved bacon fat. Cover and cook until tender. Stir in rice. Add tomatoes, chicken broth, Worcestershire sauce, salt, mace, and pepper. Bring to a boil. Cover and bake in a moderate oven, 350 degrees F., for 15 minutes. Stir in shrimp and bacon. Cover and return to oven for 10 minutes or until shrimp are done. Remove from oven, fluff with a fork, and sprinkle with parsley.

Makes 6 servings.

## Shrimp 'n Shell Casserole

1 can (10¾ ounces) cream of celery
  soup
¼ cup milk
1 tablespoon sherry

½ teaspoon curry powder
1½ cups diced cooked shrimp
2 cups cooked shell macaroni
2 tablespoons chopped parsley

In a 1-quart casserole, blend soup, milk, sherry, and curry powder. Add the remaining ingredients and blend well. Bake at 350 degrees F., for 30 minutes; stir.

Makes 2 to 4 servings.

## Savannah Stuffed Shrimp

2 pounds raw jumbo shrimp (24 to 30), fresh or frozen
1 can (6½ or 7 ounces) crabmeat, drained, flaked, and cartilage removed
¼ teaspoon salt
2 teaspoons margarine or butter
¼ cup finely chopped onion
2 tablespoons finely chopped green onion
2 tablespoons finely chopped celery
2 tablespoons finely chopped green pepper
1 tablespoon chopped parsley
1 clove garlic, minced
½ teaspoon salt
¼ teaspoon cayenne pepper
2 eggs, beaten
1 can (5⅓ ounces) evaporated milk
1 cup all-purpose flour
3 cups soft white bread crumbs
Fat for deep frying

Thaw shrimp if frozen. Shell shrimp, leaving last section of shell and tail intact. Devein, rinse, and drain dry on absorbent paper. Butterfly the shrimp by cutting along their outside curve about three quarters of the way through and carefully flattening them. Sprinkle with salt. In small saucepan, melt margarine. Add onion, green onion, celery, green pepper, parsley, and garlic. Cover and cook 5 minutes or until tender. Remove from heat. Stir in crabmeat, ½ teaspoon salt, and cayenne. Pack stuffing mixture in a band down the center of each shrimp, dividing it equally among them. Combine eggs and evaporated milk in a shallow bowl. Place flour and bread crumbs in separate pie plates. One at a time, roll the shrimp in the flour to coat evenly, dip into egg mixture, then roll in bread crumbs. Arrange shrimp on baking sheet and refrigerate one hour to firm coating. Arrange 5 or 6 shrimp in a single layer in a fry basket. Fry in deep fat, 350 degrees F., for 3 to 5 minutes or until shrimp are brown and done. Drain on absorbent paper. Keep warm in very low oven while remaining shrimp are being cooked.

Makes 6 to 8 servings.

## Shrimp Étouffée

*Étouffée is a popular method of preparing crawfish or shrimp in Louisiana. The shellfish are covered with a variety of chopped vegetables and cooked in a tightly closed pot. Vegetables may vary depending on what is available at the time.*

3 pounds raw rock shrimp or other shrimp, fresh or frozen
¼ cup margarine or butter
3 tablespoons all-purpose flour
1 cup chopped onion
½ cup chopped celery
2 tablespoons chopped green onion
¼ cup chopped green pepper
2 tablespoons chopped parsley
1 clove garlic, minced
½ cup water
1 tablespoon lemon juice
¼ teaspoon salt
¼ teaspoon cayenne pepper
3 cups cooked rice

Thaw shrimp if frozen. Peel, clean, and rinse shrimp. In 10-inch fry pan melt margarine; blend in flour. Add onion, celery, green onion, green pepper, parsley, and garlic. Cover and cook 5 minutes or until tender. Gradually add water. Stir in lemon juice, salt, and pepper. Push vegetables to one side of pan. Add shrimp to pan; spoon vegetables over shrimp. Cover and simmer for approximately 5 minutes or until shrimp are pink and tender.

Makes 4 servings.

## Shrimp à la King

1 can (4 ounces) sliced mushrooms, drained
¼ cup chopped onion
2 tablespoons butter or margarine
½ cup milk
1 can (11 ounces) Cheddar cheese soup
1 cup diced cooked shrimp
Rice or toast

In a saucepan, brown the mushrooms and cook the onion in butter until tender. Add milk, soup, and shrimp. Heat, stirring occasionally, but do not boil. Serve over rice or toast.

Makes 4 servings.

# Crab, Shrimp, and Okra Gumbo

*One of the best known Creole dishes is gumbo. Like Creole cooking itself, which is a combination of various ethnic cooking traditions, the following gumbo is a hearty mixture of several ingredients.*

1 pound blue crab meat, fresh, frozen, or pasteurized
1 pound raw, peeled, and deveined shrimp, fresh or frozen
6 tablespoons margarine or butter
6 tablespoons all-purpose flour
1 cup chopped onion
½ cup chopped green pepper
2 tablespoons chopped green onion
1 clove garlic, minced
1 quart chicken broth or bouillon

1 can (15 ounces) tomato sauce with tomato bits
1 tablespoon chopped parsley
½ teaspoon salt
½ teaspoon dried thyme leaves, crushed
¼ teaspoon cayenne pepper
1 bay leaf
Liquid hot pepper sauce, optional
1 can (1 pound) cut okra, drained
1 lemon, sliced
3 cups cooked rice

Thaw crabmeat and shrimp if frozen. Remove any remaining shell or cartilage from crabmeat. Cut large shrimp in half. In a heavy 4- to 5-quart Dutch oven, melt margarine; blend in flour. Cook, stirring constantly, over medium heat until medium brown in color, approximately 10 to 15 minutes. Add onion, green pepper, green onion, and garlic. Cook, stirring constantly, until lightly browned. Gradually stir in chicken broth. Add tomato sauce, parsley, salt, thyme, cayenne, bay leaf, and liquid hot pepper sauce. Bring to a boil; simmer 30 minutes. Add okra, lemon slices, shrimp, and crabmeat. Cover and simmer 5 minutes or until shrimp are pink and tender. Remove slices of lemon from gumbo. Serve by ladling gumbo over mounds of cooked rice in deep soup bowl.

Makes 6 servings.

## Crab Chops

*Blue crabs are abundant from New England to the Gulf of Mexico. Because of the popularity of the blue crab in so many sections of the country, various recipes for blue crab abound. It is thought that Crab Chops were originally created by Acadian cooks as a meal for days of religious fast.*

1 pound blue crab meat, fresh, frozen, or pasteurized
¼ cup margarine or butter
¼ cup all-purpose flour
½ teaspoon salt
¼ teaspoon cayenne pepper
1 cup milk
¼ cup chopped parsley
¼ cup chopped green onion
½ cup all-purpose flour
2 eggs, beaten
2 cups soft bread crumbs
¼ cup margarine or butter
¼ cup cooking oil
Lemon wedges
Tartar Sauce, see Sauces chapter

Thaw crabmeat if frozen. Remove any remaining shell or cartilage from crabmeat. In small saucepan melt ¼ cup margarine; blend in ¼ cup flour, salt, and cayenne. Gradually stir in milk. Cook and stir until thickened. Mix in crabmeat, parsley, and green onion. Cover and refrigerate for 2 hours. Divide crab mixture into 6 equal portions. Pat and shape each portion in a "chop" about 5 inches long and ½ inch thick. Place each chop in the ½ cup flour and turn to coat both sides. Dip each chop into egg and then turn in the bread crumbs to coat evenly. Refrigerate at least 30 minutes to firm coating. In heavy 12-inch fry pan, heat ¼ cup margarine and ¼ cup oil until hot but not smoking. Fry chops over moderate heat until delicately browned on both sides, about 10 minutes. Serve with lemon wedges and Tartar Sauce.

Makes 6 servings.

## Cornish Crab

*Many American dishes reflect traditional English influences. From Cornwall in western England came the pasty, a type of turnover that is filled with meat and a variety of vegetables. Sometimes potatoes were scooped out and used to wrap the pasties. Cornish Crab is a variation of those original recipes.*

| | |
|---|---|
| 1 package (6 ounces) snow crab or other crabmeat, fresh or frozen, or 1 can (6½ ounces) crabmeat | ¼ cup milk<br>½ teaspoon salt<br>¼ teaspoon pepper<br>¼ teaspoon paprika |
| 4 large baked potatoes | Parsley |
| ½ cup margarine or butter, softened | Lemon wedges |

Thaw crabmeat if frozen. Drain canned crabmeat. Remove any remaining shell or cartilage. Cut a slice off the top of each potato; scoop out potatoes, reserving shells. Mash potatoes; stir in margarine, milk, salt, and pepper. Beat until fluffy. Fold in crabmeat. Stuff potato shells with crab and potato mixture. Sprinkle stuffed potatoes with paprika. Bake in a hot oven, 400 degrees F., for 10 to 15 minutes, or until hot and lightly browned. Garnish with parsley sprigs and lemon wedges.

Makes 4 servings.

## Crabmeat Cakes

| | |
|---|---|
| 1 pound blue crab meat, fresh or pasteurized | 1 tablespoon minced parsley |
| 1 cup soft bread crumbs | 1½ teaspoons seafood seasoning |
| 1 egg, beaten | 1 teaspoon Worcestershire sauce |
| 1 tablespoon mayonnaise or salad dressing | ½ cup dry bread, cereal, or cracker crumbs |
| | Fat for frying |

Remove any pieces of shell or cartilage from crabmeat. Combine all ingredients except dry crumbs and fat. Shape into 6 cakes and roll in dry crumbs. Place cakes in a heavy frying pan containing ⅛-inch of fat, hot but not smoking. Fry at a moderate heat for 2 to 3 minutes or until brown. Turn carefully. Fry for 2 to 3 minutes longer or until cakes are brown. Drain on absorbent paper.

Makes 6 servings.

# Maryland Deviled Crab

*The blue crab was a favorite dish of the colonists. As early as the eighteenth century the Chesapeake Bay had a reputation for offering a rich bounty in crabs. Today, from the months of April to December, the Chesapeake yields more blue crabs than any other similar-sized body of water in the world. Served with sauce, Maryland Deviled Crab is a zesty dish that enhances the delicacy of the blue crab.*

1 pound crabmeat, fresh, frozen, or pasteurized
2 tablespoons margarine or butter
½ cup finely chopped onion
¼ cup finely chopped green pepper
¼ cup all-purpose flour
1 tablespoon dry mustard
1 teaspoon Worcestershire sauce
¼ teaspoon liquid hot pepper sauce

¾ teaspoon salt
¼ teaspoon pepper
Dash cayenne, optional
1¼ cups half and half
2 egg yolks, beaten
½ cup fresh bread crumbs
½ teaspoon paprika
1 tablespoon margarine or butter
Lemon wedges

Thaw crabmeat if frozen. Remove any remaining shell or cartilage. In a large skillet melt margarine. Add onion and green pepper and cook until vegetables are tender. Stir in flour, mustard, Worcestershire, liquid hot pepper sauce, salt, pepper, and cayenne. Add half and half gradually. Cook over low heat until thickened, stirring constantly. Place crab mixture into 6 crab shells or ramekins. Combine bread crumbs, paprika, and margarine. Sprinkle on top of crab mixture. Bake in a moderate oven, 350 degrees F., for 15 to 20 minutes or until hot and bread crumbs are browned. Serve with lemon wedges.

Makes 6 servings.

# Boiled Dungeness Crab

3 live Dungeness crabs
8 quarts boiling water

½ cup salt
Melted butter or margarine

Dress live crabs by inserting a table knife under the back of the top shell and prying it off. Remove spongy parts under shell (gills, stomach, and intestines) and wash the body cavity. Place in boiling salted water, cover, and return to boiling point. Simmer 15 minutes. Drain. Crack claws and legs. Serve hot with melted butter, or chill and serve with mayonnaise.

### Alternate Method

Plunge live crabs, head first, into actively boiling salted water. Cover and simmer as directed. Cool quickly and dress.

Makes 6 servings.

# Florida Stone Crab Claws à la Kennedy

*A favorite dish of President Kennedy was stone crab claws. During his administration the dish was popularized when the President vacationed at Palm Beach, Florida, which came to be known as the "Winter White House." So much did Kennedy enjoy stone crab claws that occasionally the dish was flown to Washington.*

12 to 18 Florida stone crab claws*    1 tablespoon lime juice
3 quarts water                        1 teaspoon salt

In large saucepan combine the water, salt, and lime juice. Bring to a boil. Add crab claws and simmer for 20 minutes. Remove and chill. Crack the shells in several places so that the meat can be easily removed. Serve with Sauce à la Kennedy for a real taste treat.

*Stone crab claws are almost always marketed in the cooked form. The cooking and chilling procedure above would be eliminated in such a case.

## Sauce à la Kennedy

½ cup mayonnaise               1 tablespoon prepared mustard
¼ cup steak sauce              Dash liquid hot pepper sauce
2 tablespoons lemon juice

Combine all ingredients and chill.

Makes 1 cup.

## Sitka Regal Rarebit

*During the eighteenth and nineteenth centuries there was a significant Russian presence in Alaska and along the northwestern coast of America. In 1802 the Russian America Company moved its capital from the Aleutians to Sitka, making that city the heart of Russian America. For several years Sitka flourished as a center for trade and was host to sailors and merchants who worked the harsh climate of the Pacific Northwest.*

¾ pound king crab leg meat, fresh or frozen  
3 tablespoons margarine or butter  
2 tablespoons all-purpose flour  
¼ teaspoon salt  
¼ teaspoon dry mustard  

Dash cayenne  
1 cup milk  
⅛ teaspoon Worcestershire sauce  
1 cup shredded Cheddar cheese  
1 teaspoon dry sherry  
4 slices hot buttered toast  

Thaw crab if frozen. In a skillet melt 1 tablespoon margarine. Add crab and heat until hot. In a saucepan melt remaining 2 tablespoons margarine. Blend in flour, salt, mustard, and cayenne. Add milk gradually and cook over low heat until thick, stirring constantly. Add Worcestershire and cheese. Heat until cheese melts. Stir in sherry. Place crab on top of toast. Pour sauce over crab.

Makes 2 to 4 servings.

## Quick Seafood Casserole

2 cups (two 7-ounce cans) crab-meat or combination of seafood  
2 cans (10½ ounces each) cream of mushroom soup  

½ cup milk  
1 package (4½ ounces) potato chips  
1 tablespoon butter  

Remove any shell or cartilage, being careful to keep crab in large pieces. Arrange alternate layers of crab and crushed potato chips in well-greased casserole. Pour soup, blended with milk, over top; dot with butter. Bake in a hot oven, 400 degrees F., 15 minutes or until heated through and brown.

Makes 6 servings.

# Oyster Pie Rappahannock

*Oysters were an important food of the early Americans, but up through the eighteenth century their popularity was confined mostly to coastal regions. That changed as the transportation network of the country improved. By the 1850s oysters were regularly shipped to many cities of the interior.*

1 pint oysters, standards, fresh or
    frozen
6 slices bacon
2 cups sliced fresh mushrooms
½ cup chopped onion
½ cup chopped green onion
¼ cup all-purpose flour

½ teaspoon salt
¼ teaspoon cayenne pepper
¼ cup chopped parsley
2 tablespoons lemon juice
1 tablespoon butter or margarine,
    softened
Biscuit Topping, see below

Thaw oysters if frozen. Drain oysters; dry between absorbent paper. In a 10-inch frying pan cook bacon until crisp. Remove bacon, drain, and crumble. Reserve 3 tablespoons bacon fat. Add mushrooms, onion, and green onion to reserved bacon fat. Cover and simmer 5 minutes or until tender. Blend in flour, salt, and pepper. Stir in oysters, bacon, parsley, and lemon juice. Grease a 9-inch pie plate with softened margarine. Turn oyster mixture into pie plate. Cover with biscuit topping. Score biscuit topping to make a design on top. Bake in hot oven, 400 degrees F., for 20 to 25 minutes or until biscuit topping is lightly browned. Cut into wedges.

Makes 6 servings.

## Biscuit Topping

1½ cups all-purpose flour
2¼ teaspoons baking powder
¼ teaspoon salt

3 tablespoons margarine or butter
½ cup milk

Sift dry ingredients together. Cut in margarine until it is like coarse crumbs. Add milk all at once. Mix just to a soft dough. Turn onto lightly floured surface. Knead gently 5 to 6 strokes. Shape into a ball. Roll out to a 9-inch circle to fit on top of pie plate.

# Oyster Loaf

*Oysters are harvested along the East Coast and Gulf of Mexico. Because of the relative abundance of oysters, Americans have created a wide variety of ways of preparing them. The Oyster Loaf was one of the most popular recipes for oysters throughout America during the nineteenth century.*

1 pint oysters, standards, fresh or frozen
½ teaspoon salt
⅛ teaspoon pepper
2 eggs, beaten
¼ cup milk
¾ cup all-purpose flour
2 cups soft bread crumbs

½ cup margarine or butter, melted
2 loaves French bread, 15 inches long and 3 inches wide
Fat for deep frying
½ cup tartar sauce
1½ cups shredded lettuce
18 thin tomato slices

Thaw oysters if frozen. Drain oysters; dry between absorbent paper. Sprinkle with salt and pepper. Combine eggs and milk. Roll oysters in flour, dip into egg mixture, then roll in bread crumbs to coat evenly. Refrigerate at least 30 minutes to firm coating. Slice bread loaves in half horizontally. Pull out the inside soft crumb from bottom and top halves of bread. Brush the bread shells inside with melted margarine. Place bread shells on baking sheet and bake in a moderate oven, 350 degrees F., 3 to 5 minutes to warm and crisp. Place oysters in a single layer in a fry basket. Fry in deep fat, 350 degrees F., for 2 to 3 minutes. Drain on absorbent paper. Spread inside of bread shells with tartar sauce. Place shredded lettuce in the bottom halves of the loaves. Arrange tomato slices on lettuce, and fried oysters on top of the tomatoes. Cover with top halves of the loaves of bread. Cut each loaf into 3 portions.

Makes 6 servings.

## Heritage Scalloped Oysters

1 pint oysters
2 cups coarse cracker crumbs
½ cup melted margarine or butter
½ teaspoon salt

⅛ teaspoon pepper
¼ teaspoon Worcestershire sauce
1 cup milk

Thaw oysters if frozen. Drain oysters. Combine cracker crumbs, margarine, salt, and pepper. Reserve ⅓ mixture for topping. Place another ⅓ of crumb mixture in a well-greased 1-quart casserole; cover with a layer of oysters. Repeat layers. Add Worcestershire sauce to milk, and pour over contents of casserole. Top with reserved ⅓ crumb mixture. Bake in a moderate oven, 350 degrees F., for 30 minutes or until thoroughly heated.

Makes 6 servings.

## Puget Sound Clams in Shells

*Fish and shellfish provided a significant amount of food for the Indians of the West Coast. For the early settlers of Puget Sound, the sea provided the only reliable source of food.*

2 cans (6½ or 7 ounces each)
   canned clams, minced or
   chopped
12 ounces shell macaroni
2 or 3 garlic cloves, minced

½ cup grated Parmesan cheese
⅓ cup chopped parsley
¼ cup melted margarine or butter
½ teaspoon salt
⅛ teaspoon pepper

Drain clams and reserve liquid. Cook macaroni according to package directions. Meanwhile, in a 2-quart saucepan, cook clam liquid with garlic over low heat until reduced to one half. Drain macaroni well. Combine macaroni, clams and liquid, cheese, parsley, margarine, salt, and pepper. Heat. If desired, portion the mixture into six 8-ounce individual baking shells or ramekins. Garnish with additional Parmesan cheese and broil for 2 to 3 minutes until lightly browned.

Makes 6 servings.

## Pilgrims Clam Pie

*During their first year on the North American continent, the Pilgrims learned to depend on the sea as a major source of food. It saved many from starvation. Clams were one of the most easily obtainable foods of the sea, for they could be found in the mud flats at low tide. Even as the colony grew and other food sources became available, the clam continued to be a major part of the Pilgrims' diet, showing up in a variety of recipes.*

3 dozen shell clams or 3 cans (8 ounces each) minced clams, undrained
1½ cups water
¼ cup margarine or butter
½ cup sliced fresh mushrooms
2 tablespoons minced onion
¼ cup all-purpose flour
⅛ teaspoon liquid hot pepper sauce
¼ teaspoon dry mustard
¼ teaspoon salt
⅛ teaspoon white pepper
1 cup reserved clam liquor
1 cup half and half
1 tablespoon lemon juice
2 tablespoons chopped parsley
2 tablespoons chopped pimiento
Pastry for a 1-crust 9-inch pie, any recipe
1 egg, beaten

Wash clam shells thoroughly. Place clams in a large pot with water. Bring to a boil and simmer for 8 to 10 minutes or until clams open. Remove clams from shell and cut into fourths. Reserve 1 cup clam liquor. (Or, if using canned clams, drain and reserve 1 cup liquor.) In a skillet melt margarine. Add mushrooms and onion and cook until tender. Stir in flour, mustard, liquid hot pepper sauce, salt, and pepper. Gradually add clam liquor and half and half. Cook, stirring constantly, until thick. Stir in lemon juice, parsley, pimiento, and clams. Pour mixture into a 9-inch round deep-dish pie plate (about 2 inches deep). Roll out pastry dough and place on top of mixture in pie plate; secure dough to the rim of the pie plate by crimping. Vent pastry. Brush with beaten egg. Bake in a hot oven, 375 degrees F., for 25 to 30 minutes or until pastry is browned.

Makes 4 to 6 servings.

# Razor Clam Crumb Pie

### *Crust*

2 cups soft bread crumbs
1 tablespoon grated onion
¼ teaspoon celery salt
½ teaspoon salt

Dash sage
Dash pepper
¼ cup butter or other fat

Combine all ingredients and mix well. Press into an 8- or 9-inch baking pan. Bake in a moderate oven, 375 degrees F., 25 minutes, or until brown.

### *Filling*

1 can (7 ounces) minced razor
    clams, undrained
6 tablespoons all-purpose flour
6 tablespoons butter or other fat
1 cup clam liquor and water as
    necessary to bring to full
    measure

1 cup milk
½ teaspoon salt
Dash pepper
¼ teaspoon celery salt
2 tablespoons butter, melted
¼ cup dry bread crumbs

Drain clams, reserving liquor. Melt fat and blend in flour. Add liquid gradually; cook until thick and smooth, stirring constantly. Add seasonings and clams. Pour into baked crust. Combine butter and crumbs; sprinkle over top. Bake in a hot oven, 425 degrees F., 12 minutes, or until brown.

Makes 2 to 4 servings.

## Family Clam Bake

| | |
|---|---|
| 2½ gallons scrubbed clams, in the shell | 2 dozen small white potatoes |
| 1 dozen ears corn, in husks | 1 pound butter |

Dig a hole approximately 4 feet square and 8 to 10 inches deep; fill with rocks. (Don't use rocks that have been lying underwater—they may explode when heated.) Provide plenty of firewood and wet seaweed; avoid old or dead weed as this will impart a bad flavor to the food. Build a fire over the prepared bed of rocks and continue adding fuel for 1 to 2 hours until the stones are thoroughly heated and a good bed of embers is formed. Remove any smoking pieces of wood and cover rocks and embers with at least 4 inches of wet seaweed. Without any loss of time, spread out the food on the bed of seaweed and cover with an additional 4 inches of seaweed. Cover the hole with an old canvas so as to retain the steam that cooks the food. Keep covered for about 40 minutes or until the potatoes are cooked.

Along the seacoast, the heated stones are sometimes placed in a hole scooped out of sand to a depth of 12 to 18 inches. A layer of hot sand from around the fire may be used instead of canvas for covering the top layer of seaweed. Cheesecloth or similar lightweight material is sometimes used to cover the food, being placed between the layers of seaweed.

The clams will open during the cooking. The loose cover around the neck of the clam should be removed. Dip the clam into hot melted butter, using the dark neck as a handle. Bite the body meat off and discard the neck. By eating near the cooking place, food may be kept covered and hot until used.

Makes 12 servings.

## Clam Fritters

| | |
|---|---|
| 1 pint clams (2 7-ounce cans), undrained | Clam liquor and enough milk to make ⅔ cup |
| 1 cup all-purpose flour | 2 eggs, well beaten |
| 1 teaspoon salt | Dash pepper |
| 1½ teaspoons baking powder | |

Drain clams and chop, reserving liquor. Sift dry ingredients together. Measure clam liquor, adding milk if necessary to bring to ⅔ cup in all. Combine this liquid with the eggs and clams. Add to the dry mixture and mix well. If pan frying, drop by tablespoons into hot fat (¼ inch deep), and brown on each side. If deep fat frying is used, drop by tablespoons into the fat (350 degrees F.) and brown on each side. Be sure to turn them only once. Drain on absorbent paper. Garnish and serve hot, plain or with a sauce.

Makes 2 to 4 servings.


## Sea Scallops—in Shells

*Over the years there has been a growing demand for scallops in North America. Scallops may be baked, grilled, and battered and fried and, as the following recipe shows, served in shells.*

1½ pounds sea or other scallops, fresh or frozen
1 cup water or ½ cup dry white wine and ½ cup water
1 teaspoon salt
¼ cup margarine or butter
½ pound small mushrooms, sliced
⅓ cup finely chopped celery
⅓ cup sliced green onion
3 tablespoons all-purpose flour
Dash of white pepper
1¼ cups half and half
1 tablespoon lemon juice
Dash liquid hot pepper sauce, optional
2 tablespoons chopped pimiento, optional
1 cup very fine soft bread crumbs

Thaw scallops if frozen. Rinse with cold water to remove any shell particles. Cook scallops in water or wine and water and ½ teaspoon salt until tender, about 5 minutes. Drain; save cooking liquid. Cook liquid until it is reduced to ¾ cup. Cut large scallops in half. Melt 3 tablespoons margarine or butter in saucepan. Add mushrooms; cook until tender and moisture evaporates. Add celery and onion; cook 2 to 3 minutes. Stir in flour, remaining ½ teaspoon salt, and pepper. Add half and half and cooking liquid; cook until thickened, stirring constantly. Stir in lemon juice and liquid hot pepper sauce, if used. Add scallops and pimiento; heat. Spoon into 6 to 8 shells or individual baking dishes. Melt remaining 1 tablespoon margarine or butter and mix with bread crumbs. Sprinkle around edges of each dish. Bake in hot oven, 400 degrees F., 10 to 20 minutes.

Makes 6 to 8 servings.

## Deluxe Baked Scallops

2 pounds scallops, fresh or frozen
1 quart boiling water
2 tablespoons salt
1 can (10½ ounces) cream of
    mushroom soup
¼ cup dairy sour cream
2 tablespoons frozen orange juice
    concentrate

2 tablespoons chopped parsley
1 tablespoon lemon juice
1 tablespoon grated onion
½ teaspoon salt
¼ cup dry bread crumbs
1 tablespoon butter or margarine,
    melted

Thaw frozen scallops. Rinse scallops with cold water to remove any shell particles. Place in boiling salted water. Cover and simmer for 2 to 3 minutes, depending on size. Drain. Cut large scallops in half. Combine all ingredients except crumbs and butter. Place in 6 well-greased individual shells or 6-ounce custard cups. Place shells on a baking pan, 15×10×1 inches. Combine crumbs and butter. Sprinkle over scallop mixture. Bake in a moderate oven, 350 degrees F., for 20 to 25 minutes or until brown.

Makes 6 servings.

## Baked Stuffed Scallops

1 pound scallops, rinsed and pat-
    ted dry
½ cup butter
1 cup bread crumbs
1 small onion, finely chopped
1 small clove garlic, crushed
¼ cup finely chopped parsley
1 tablespoon finely chopped
    tarragon

1 tablespoon finely chopped basil
¼ teaspoon salt
¼ teaspoon pepper
¼ teaspoon sugar
¼ teaspoon Worcestershire sauce
1 tablespoon lemon juice
1 teaspoon anchovy paste,
    optional

Arrange scallops in 4 well-buttered ramekins. Melt butter in skillet. Place bread crumbs in bowl and toss well with 3 tablespoons of melted butter. Put all other ingredients into skillet with remaining butter. Saute mixture over low heat for 5 minutes. Divide among the ramekins and stir to combine with scallops. Top with bread crumb mixture and bake in preheated oven at 400 degrees F., for 5 to 8 minutes or until brown.

Makes 4 servings.

## Crawfish "Skandia"

15 live crawfish
1½ quarts water
1 teaspoon salt
2 sugar cubes
5 bundles fresh dill
½ tablespoon dill seeds
1 lemon, cut into 8 wedges
1 bottle (8 or 12 ounces) beer
1 cup mayonnaise

½ tablespoon Dijon-style mustard
½ tablespoon paprika
White pepper, to taste
2 drops Worcestershire sauce
1 tablespoon dried dillweed
Crushed ice
Aquavit (or vodka), ice cold
Beer

Combine water and salt and bring to a boil. Add the sugar cubes, 3 bundles of dill, and the dill seeds. Cook for a minute then add 1 lemon wedge and the bottle of beer. When water comes to second boil, drop the live crawfish in the stock and cook at a slow boil for 4 minutes. Remove the pot from the stove. Remove the crawfish from the stock and place in refrigerator to cool. While the crawfish are cooling, make a dill sauce (dip) in the following manner: combine mayonnaise, mustard, paprika, white pepper, Worcestershire sauce, dillweed, the juice from 1 lemon wedge, and a full teaspoon of fresh finely chopped dill. Stir well and chill.

To serve, arrange the crawfish on a platter of crushed ice with the dill sauce in the middle. Garnish with the remaining fresh dill and 6 lemon wedges. Serve with a shot of ice cold (from the freezer) aquavit or vodka with beer as a chaser.

Makes 2 servings.

## Mousse of Crawfish

3 dozen crawfish
1 cup white wine
2 tablespoons brandy
3 tablespoons all-purpose flour
2 tablespoons soft butter
1 ounce gelatin
1 cup heavy cream
Water, for dissolving gelatin
2 carrots

2 onions
1 clove garlic
2 crushed tomatoes
6 scallions
⅛ teaspoon thyme
1 bay leaf, crushed
½ teaspoon whole black pepper
Salt, to taste

Chop carrots, onions, garlic, crushed tomatoes, and scallions. Saute in butter with thyme, bay leaf, whole black pepper, and salt. Stir-fry crawfish in a wok with hot oil and add sauteed vegetables, wine, and brandy. Cook for 7 minutes. Remove crawfish and vegetables and reduce the pan juice slowly for another 7 minutes.

Blend flour and butter together well, add to the pan sauce, and let and let cook slowly for 15 to 20 minutes. Skim off the impurities. (This is called Sauce Nantua and should be set aside.)

Twist tails off crawfish and remove the meat. (Three dozen crawfish should yield about 1 cup of meat.) Put meat and vegetables in a blender and puree. Add 1 cup of Sauce Nantua to puree and mix well. Add the gelatin, dissolved in a minimum amount of water, to the mixture.

Let cool until mixture begins to thicken; then, slowly add 1 cup heavy cream (whipped, but not too stiff) and mix well. Pour into a mold and refrigerate to set. Decorate as desired.

Makes 2 to 4 servings.

## Pâté Chaud of Crawfish Forrestière

36 raw crawfish
2 egg whites
⅛ teaspoon salt
Fresh ground pepper, to taste
Dash of nutmeg
½ cup heavy cream

Puff dough (any recipe)
Sauteed mushrooms (¼ cup or
    more if desired)
Parsley
Egg wash (beaten yolks with
    water)

Remove tails from 36 raw crawfish. Puree crawfish meat. (Yield will be about 1 cup.) Pour into bowl and add the 2 egg whites. Mix well with spatula. Add the salt, pepper, and nutmeg. Slowly stir in the heavy cream and mix gently to evenly distribute all ingredients.

Make the puff dough and roll out into any shape desired. Spread half of the crawfish mixture onto half of the pastry dough. Be sure to leave the edges clean. Top with sauteed mushrooms (seasoned with parsley and other desired spices) and then add the remainder of the crawfish mixture on top. Fold dough over the top and press edges together. Brush with egg wash (the yolks beaten with enough water to obtain a thin, spreadable consistency). Bake at 375 degrees F. for 20 minutes.

Makes 4 servings.

# Écrevisse Polynaise

3 dozen crawfish tails, shelled
½ teaspoon curry powder
½ orange, diced
½ apple, diced
½ pear, diced
1 banana, sliced
1 ounce marmalade
1 ounce mango chutney

1 ounce coconut shreds
½ onion, chopped fine
6 mushrooms, sliced
2 ounces dry white wine
½ cup chicken consomme
¼ cup butter or margarine
¼ cup milk

Saute onions and mushrooms until tender but not brown. Add the remaining ingredients and saute for 6 to 10 minutes, reserving the milk and consomme.

Combine milk and consomme and heat to simmering. Thicken this mixture with roux [see below] as desired and add to the pan with the crawfish tails. Simmer all together for another 4 minutes and serve over rice.

Roux is a fat and flour mixture used for thickening sauces and gravies. Many French cooks make this up ahead of time and store in refrigerator in a closed jar. Fat is heated and flour stirred in until a smooth, bubbling mixture is obtained. Add to sauce a little at a time and cook until the desired thickness is obtained. If sauce becomes too thick, dilute with a little water or milk.

Makes 2 to 4 servings.

## Cleaning Octopus and Squid

These fish are very similar in shape, taste, and treatment. They both have a body that can be formed into a natural sack for stuffing if so desired, and an effective ink-ejecting mechanism. The transparent cartilage must be removed from both fish before they are ready for cooking. This cartilage becomes the cuttlebone you often see in birdcages, after a period of heating and drying.

To prepare these fish, remove the anal portion, beaklike mouth, and the eyes. Be extra careful not to puncture the ink sac which lies close to the eyes. With small fish, this job may be done with scissors. If the fish happen to be large (2 pounds each, and up), you will need a sharp knife to allow you to penetrate far enough to slip them inside out. Remove the yellowish pouch, all attached membranes, and discard. Wash in cold running water to remove any gelatinous matter.

When using frozen inkfish, check instructions on the package for the proper handling methods and also note if the fish have been cleaned. If not, thaw and follow the directions.

If you wish, remove the ink sacs and reserve for sauces. The ink is used in many dishes and may be frozen for future use. It gives color, flavor, and body to many sauces.

## Squid Fritters Americana

1½ pounds whole squid, fresh or frozen  
Vegetable oil

Canned or fresh cranberry sauce or cranberry orange relish

### Batter

⅔ cup all-purpose flour  
½ cup water  
1 tablespoon cornstarch  
1 teaspoon baking powder

Dash paprika  
3 egg whites, slightly beaten  
Salt, white pepper to taste

Thaw frozen squid. Clean squid according to the procedure above. Cook mantles in boiling, salted water 1 hour or until tender; drain. Cut mantles into quarters.

Heat oil to 375 degrees F. Combine batter ingredients. Dip squid into batter and fry in oil until golden brown (about 2 to 4 minutes). Serve hot with cranberry sauce or relish.

Makes 4 servings.

## Stuffed Squid Monterey

*Although a squid fishery was begun in Monterey Bay in California during the early 1860s, squid remained popular mostly among Americans of Oriental or Mediterranean descent. Only within the last few years has squid started gaining general acceptance in America. To expand the appeal of squid, many recipes today are using American ingredients.*

| | |
|---|---|
| 2 pounds whole squid, fresh or frozen | ⅔ cup chopped parsley |
| 1 cup chopped onion | 4 teaspoons dry sherry |
| ⅔ cup chopped carrot | ¼ teaspoon salt |
| ½ cup margarine or butter, melted | ⅛ teaspoon pepper |
| 4 cups fresh bread crumbs | Margarine or butter for frying |

Thaw squid if frozen. Cut through arms near the eyes. With the thumb and forefinger, squeeze out the inedible beak which will be located near the cut. Chop tentacles and reserve for stuffing. Feel inside the mantle for chitinous pen. Firmly grasp pen and attached viscera; remove from mantle. Wash mantle thoroughly and drain. Cook onion, carrot, and chopped tentacles in melted margarine until tender. Stir in crumbs, parsley, sherry, salt, and pepper. Stuff squid loosely. Close opening with small skewer or toothpick if desired. Fry over moderately high heat in margarine or half margarine and half oil for 3 to 4 minutes; turn carefully and fry 3 to 4 minutes on other side just until squid is cooked.

Makes 6 servings.

## Squid Pie

3 pounds whole squid, fresh or
    frozen
2 tablespoons salad oil
1 cup canned French fried onion
    rings
1 can (10½ ounces) cream of celery
    soup

1 can (4 ounces) mushrooms,
    drained
1 teaspoon Worcestershire sauce
Dash pepper
¾ cup mashed potatoes
1 tablespoon chopped parsley
Paprika

Thaw frozen squid. Clean squid according to procedure above. Cook mantles in boiling, salted water 1 hour or until tender; drain. Cut mantles into small pieces.

Cook onion rings in oil until tender; add squid, soup, mushrooms, Worcestershire sauce, and pepper. Spread mixture over bottom of well-greased 10-inch pie pan. Top with mashed potatoes. Sprinkle with parsley and paprika. Bake at 450 degrees F. for 40 minutes or until brown.

Makes 6 servings.

## Garden Style Squid

2 pounds whole squid, fresh or
    frozen
2 tablespoons oil
2 medium carrots, grated
1 medium onion, grated

2 large tomatoes, chopped
1½ cups water
Thyme to taste
Salt, pepper to taste
½ tablespoon all-purpose flour

Thaw frozen squid. Clean squid according to procedure above. Cook mantles in boiling, salted water 1 hour or until tender; drain. Cut mantles into pieces.

Saute carrots and onion in oil. Add tomatoes and water and simmer 15 minutes. Season with thyme, salt, and pepper. Stir in flour with vegetables; add squid. Cook additional 5 minutes. Serve hot or cold.

Makes 4 servings.

# Microwaving Seafood

# How to Cook Fish in a Microwave Oven

While the microwave oven seems to have its limitations in cooking certain kinds of raw meat, it does such an excellent job on raw fish that it would appear to have been made exclusively for this purpose. Fish retain their natural juices and delicate flavors (this is due to the quick cooking process), making them one of the best foods you can cook in a microwave oven. Here are a few tips on microwaving fish:

Frozen fish should be thawed before cooking, but only until the fish can be handled easily, and still quite cold.

Brush seafood or fish inside and out with butter or margarine before cooking.

When microwaving several portions of fish at one time, try to select pieces that are uniform in size and thickness.

If thicker pieces must be cooked with thinner ones, place the thicker pieces along the outer edge of the baking dish to promote even cooking.

If you cook another food at the same time, cover the fish with a plastic wrap to avoid intermingling of flavors.

Be sure the fish are firm when placed in the oven, and to avoid breaking up the pieces, don't turn them after they have been placed in the oven.

Determining when fish is done is critical in microwaving, since a few seconds in a microwave oven can make a considerable difference.

Also, since the wattage of various microwave ovens varies, the only way to test the doneness of fish is to check it before the end of the recommended cooking time. Just as when cooked by conventional methods, fish and seafood will flake easily when tested with a fork. Food temperature rises after being cooked in a microwave. Therefore, let large seafood dishes, such as baked fish, stand covered after cooking to evenly distribute the heat.

Breaded and battered fish sticks and portions cannot be cooked in a microwave oven; however, they can be precooked by conventional methods and reheated in the microwave.

Finally, do not attempt to cook fish or seafood in a microwave oven if they have been prepared for deep frying.

## Seafood Gumbo

½ pound raw, peeled, and cleaned shrimp, fresh or frozen
½ pound blue crab meat, fresh, frozen, or pasteurized
⅓ cup butter or other fat
⅔ cup chopped green onion and tops
2 cups sliced fresh okra or 1 package (10 ounces) frozen okra, sliced

½ cup chopped celery
2 cloves garlic, finely chopped
1½ teaspoons salt
½ teaspoon pepper
¼ teaspoon sugar
¼ teaspoon crushed thyme
1 whole bay leaf
6 drops liquid hot pepper sauce
2 cans (1 pound each) tomatoes
1½ cups cooked rice

Thaw frozen seafood. Remove any shell or cartilage from crabmeat. Combine butter, onion, okra, celery, garlic, and seasonings in a 3-quart bowl. Cover. Cook 12 minutes in microwave oven, stirring occasionally during cooking to separate okra. Add tomatoes, shrimp, and crabmeat; cover. Cook 16 minutes stirring occasionally during cooking. Remove bay leaf. Place ¼ cup rice in each of six soup bowls. Fill with gumbo.

Makes 6 servings.

## Shrimp Creole

2 tablespoons butter or margarine
¾ cup chopped green pepper
1 cup chopped onion
1 cup chopped celery
1½ tablespoons all-purpose flour
1 can (14½ ounces) tomatoes
1 teaspoon sugar

5 to 6 drops liquid hot pepper sauce
Dash powdered bay leaf
1 teaspoon salt
⅛ teaspoon pepper
1 pound shrimp, shelled and cleaned

In a 2- to 2½-quart casserole melt butter in microwave oven, about 1½ minutes. Stir in green pepper, onion, and celery; cook 4 minutes or until vegetables are barely tender; stir vegetables at least once during this time. Sprinkle vegetables with flour and stir to blend. Add tomatoes and cook 3 minutes; stir well and cook 3 minutes longer. Add sugar, liquid hot pepper sauce, bay leaf, salt, and pepper; blend the seasonings into the mixture. Add shrimp. Heat about 6 minutes, stirring lightly at 2-minute intervals. Correct the seasoning if necessary. Serve over cooked rice.

Makes 4 servings.

## Curried Shrimp and Potato Puff Casserole

1 cup (8 ounces) dairy sour cream
1 can (10½ ounce) cream of
    shrimp soup, undiluted
½ to 1 teaspoon curry powder
1 package (20 ounces) frozen
    ready-to-cook shrimp
1 package (1 pound) frozen shred-
    ded potato nuggets

1 tablespoon minced onion
¼ cup chopped green olives
2 tablespoons chopped ripe olives
Chow mein noodles or rice,
    enough for 4 to 6 servings
Mandarin orange sections, drained
Slivered almonds

Stir sour cream, soup, and curry powder together in 2-quart casserole. Add the shrimp and potato nuggets, stirring well. Cover. Place in microwave oven and cook 18 to 20 minutes, stirring carefully but well after 8 minutes.

Carefully stir onion and olives into the hot mixture. Cover and let stand for 5 to 7 minutes. Serve over crisp chow mein noodles and garnish as desired with Mandarin orange sections and slivered almonds.

Makes 4 to 6 servings.

# Jambalaya

1 cup diced cooked ham
½ cup chopped green pepper
½ cup chopped onion
1 garlic clove, minced
2 tablespoons butter or margarine
1 can (10¾ ounces) tomato soup
⅓ cup water

1 can (6¾ ounces) shrimp, drained
1 medium bay leaf, crushed, or ¼
    teaspoon, ground
¼ teaspoon crushed oregano
⅛ teaspoon salt
Dash pepper
1½ cups cooked rice

Place ham, green pepper, onion, garlic, and butter in a 3-quart casserole. Place in microwave oven and cook 5 to 6 minutes or until vegetables are tender. Stir in the soup, water, shrimp, and seasonings. Continue cooking in microwave oven for 4 minutes. Stir in the rice and continue to cook 4 to 6 minutes more, or until bubbly.

Makes 4 servings.

# Turban of Sole

2 tablespoons butter or margarine
½ cup (about 1 stalk) finely
    chopped celery
¼ cup finely chopped onion or 1
    tablespoon instant minced
    onion
1½ teaspoons parsley flakes or 3
    tablespoons minced fresh
    parsley

¼ teaspoon chervil, optional
1 teaspoon lemon juice
Dash white or black pepper
Dash thyme
1½ cups (1½ slices) soft bread
    cubes
1 pound sole fillets, fresh or frozen, thawed

In a 1-quart bowl or casserole, combine butter, celery, onion, seasonings, and lemon juice. Cook, covered, 3 minutes, stirring once. Mix bread cubes with mixture. Butter four 6-ounce custard cups. Line sides and bottoms with thin pieces of fish, reserving small scraps for top. (You may have to cut thick pieces in half.) Evenly divide stuffing between the 4 custard cups (about ½ cup each). Top with any leftover pieces of fish. Place custard cups on a dinner plate, microwave for 4 minutes or until fish flakes easily. When done, with another dinner plate placed on top of the custard cups, using both hands, invert plates with the custard cups between them. Let stand covered while making sauce.

### Sauce

Half of 10½-ounce can cream of mushroom soup
1 tablespoon milk or cream

1 tablespoon chopped pimiento or ripe olives

Combine all ingredients for sauce. Cook, uncovered, for 1 minute and 30 seconds or until mixture bubbles. Remove top plate and custard cups. Spoon sauce over turbans and serve.

The stuffing can also be used to stuff four 8- to 10-ounce whole fish. You can use preseasoned bread cubes and eliminate seasonings in recipe.

Makes 4 servings.

# Sauces, Marinades,
# Dips, Dressings, Stuffings, Etc.

## Sauces

A good sauce is often thought of as the final touch to a dish. This special blend of ingredients not only enhances the flavor of foods but also the appearance. Sauces should always be chosen to complement foods with which they are served.

## Drawn Butter

Many seafood recipes call for drawn butter. It is best made by bringing butter to a boil, letting it settle down, and skimming off any foam on top. Then, pour off the liquid—"Drawn Butter"—and discard the settlings.

## Drawn Butter Sauce

4 tablespoons butter, divided
2 tablespoons all-purpose flour
½ teaspoon salt

⅛ teaspoon pepper
1 teaspoon lemon juice
1 cup hot water or fish stock

Melt 2 tablespoons butter, add flour and seasonings, blend in hot water. Cook until thick. Add lemon juice and stir in remaining butter in small bits until melted and blended. Serve warm.

Makes 1 cup.

## Vinegar Sauce

1 cup white vinegar
1 small onion, very thinly sliced

Salt to taste
Coarse ground pepper

Mix ingredients together. Let stand several hours at room temperature before serving.

Makes 1 cup.

## Egg Sauce

¼ cup margarine or butter
⅓ cup all-purpose flour
1 teaspoon dry mustard
1 teaspoon salt
⅛ teaspoon white pepper

4 cups half and half
½ teaspoon liquid hot pepper
     sauce
5 hard-cooked eggs, chopped
2 tablespoons chopped parsley

In a saucepan melt margarine. Stir in flour, mustard, salt, and pepper. Add half and half gradually, and cook over low heat until thick and smooth, stirring constantly. Stir in liquid hot pepper sauce, chopped eggs, and parsley.

Makes 4 cups.

## Hollandaise Sauce

*Some say Hollandaise sauce is French in origin; others say it is Dutch. Although the origin of Hollandaise sauce may be in dispute, one thing is clear—it is an excellent sauce for various types of seafood.*

## Blender Hollandaise Sauce

3 egg yolks
2 tablespoons lemon juice

Dash cayenne pepper
½ cup margarine or butter

Place egg yolks, lemon juice, and cayenne pepper in blender container. Cover; quickly turn blender on and off. Heat margarine until melted and almost boiling. Turn blender on high speed; slowly pour in margarine, blending util thick and fluffy, about 30 seconds. Heat over warm, not hot, water until ready to serve.

Makes 1 cup.

## White Sauce

2 tablespoons butter
2 tablespoons all-purpose flour
1 cup milk

½ teaspoon salt
Dash of white pepper

Melt butter over low heat. Mix in flour. Cook, stirring until mixture is smooth and bubbly. Add milk gradually, stirring constantly until thickened. Add seasonings. Cook a few minutes longer for best flavor.

Makes 1 cup.

### *Variations on a Theme*

a. Egg Sauce: Add 1 or 2 chopped, hard-cooked eggs to 1 cup White Sauce. If desired, 2 tablespoons chopped parsley may be added.
b. Cheese Sauce: Add ½ cup grated Cheddar cheese to 1 cup White Sauce.
c. Tomato Sauce: Use 1 cup tomato juice in place of milk in White Sauce.
d. Spicy Sauce: Simmer 1¼ cups tomato juice with 1 slice onion, 2 cloves, and 1 bay leaf. Strain. Use this liquid in place of milk in White Sauce.
e. Easy Tomato Sauce: Use 1 6-ounce can of tomato cocktail and add water to make 1 cup. Use in place of milk in White Sauce.

Any of these may be used with cooked cut-up meat, fish, or vegetables. Sauces change leftovers to plannedovers.

## Parsley Sauce

⅔ cup oil
⅓ cup wine vinegar
1 teaspoon thyme

½ teaspoon salt
½ teaspoon black pepper
1 tablespoon chopped parsley

Combine all ingredients in a saucepan. Use as basting sauce and dip.

Makes 1 cup.

## Lemon Sauce I

½ cup butter                          ¼ cup lemon juice

Melt butter. Blend in lemon juice; serve warm.

Makes ¾ cup.

## Lemon Sauce II

¼ cup mayonnaise                     1 teaspoon grated lemon rind
2 tablespoons all-purpose flour      1 tablespoon chopped parsley
1 cup milk                           ¼ teaspoon salt
1 tablespoon lemon juice

Blend mayonnaise and flour in saucepan. Stir in milk and cook until thickened. Slowly add lemon juice. Stir in grated rind, parsley, and salt.

Makes 1¼ cups.

## Lemon Garlic Sauce

½ cup butter                         3 tablespoons lemon juice
¼ clove garlic, minced               4 teaspoons sugar
2 teaspoons all-purpose flour        ½ teaspoon salt
⅓ cup water                          Dash of cayenne

Melt butter, add garlic, and saute quickly. Take pan from heat, add flour, and stir to blend smoothly. Return to low heat, add water, lemon juice, sugar, salt, and cayenne. Cook until slightly thick, stirring constantly. Use as a basting sauce and dip.

Makes 1 cup.

## Lemon Mustard Sauce

¼ cup butter or margarine      1 teaspoon salt
¼ cup all-purpose flour        2 cups hot water
1 or 2 teaspoons prepared mustard    2 tablespoons lemon juice

Melt butter or margarine in saucepan. Add flour, prepared mustard, and salt, blending well. Gradually add hot water; cook over low heat, stirring constantly, until mixture thickens. Add lemon juice; cook 3 minutes longer.

Makes 1½ cups.

## Fluffy Lemon Sauce

2 tablespoons butter or margarine    1¼ cups milk
2 tablespoons all-purpose flour      ½ cup mayonnaise or salad
½ teaspoon salt                          dressing
¼ teaspoon paprika                   2 teaspoons lemon juice

Melt butter in a 1-quart saucepan. Blend in flour, salt, and paprika. Add milk gradually and cook, stirring constantly, until thickened. Stir in mayonnaise and lemon juice. Heat, but do not boil. Serve warm over poached or baked fish.

Makes 1¾ cups.

## Mustard Sauce

2 tablespoons butter           ¼ cup prepared mustard
1 tablespoon all-purpose flour ½ cup dairy sour cream

Melt butter over low heat. Blend in flour and mustard. Cook until thickened, stirring constantly. Stir in sour cream and heat.

Makes ¾ cup.

## Cool Blender Sauce

¾ cup mayonnaise or salad
   dressing
1 egg
3 tablespoons lemon juice
1 teaspoon salt
1 teaspoon sugar
1 teaspoon instant minced onion

1 teaspoon prepared mustard
2 drops liquid hot pepper sauce
Dash pepper
¾ cup salad oil
⅓ cup chopped parsley
1 tablespoon horseradish
1 clove garlic, minced

Place first nine ingredients in blender. Cover, blend a few seconds; add oil gradually and continue to blend until thick and smooth. Add parsley, horseradish, and garlic, and blend until smooth. Serve with smoked fish.

Makes approximately 2¼ cups.

## Anchovy Sauce

1 can (2 ounces) anchovy fillets,
   minced
1 garlic clove, crushed

Juice of 1 lemon
1 cup tomato juice
½ cup butter

In a saucepan, combine half of the anchovy fillets and the rest of ingredients. Simmer until butter is melted. Use as basting sauce and dip.

Makes 1½ cups.

## Dill Sauce

1 cup mayonnaise
½ tablespoon Dijon-style mustard
½ tablespoon paprika
2 drops Worcestershire sauce

1 tablespoon dried dillweed
Juice from ⅛ lemon
1 teaspoon finely chopped fresh
   dill

Stir well and chill.

Makes 1 cup.

## Pimento Cheese Sauce

¼ cup butter or margarine
3 tablespoons chopped green
   pepper
¼ cup all-purpose flour
2 cups milk

1½ cups shredded Cheddar cheese
⅓ cup sliced mushrooms,
   optional
2 tablespoons chopped pimiento
½ teaspoon salt

Melt butter or margarine in top of double boiler. Add green pepper;
cook over boiling water until tender, about 2 minutes. Blend in flour.
Add milk and cook, stirring occasionally, until thickened. Stir in
cheese, sliced mushrooms, pimiento, and salt. Continue cooking
and stirring until cheese is melted.

                                       Makes approximately 2½ cups.

## Roquefort Sauce

Into a jar with tight-fitting lid, put:

1½ cups oil
¾ cup crumbled Roquefort cheese
½ cup lemon juice

1 teaspoon salt
1 teaspoon paprika
½ teaspoon white pepper

Shake until well blended. Use as basting sauce and dip.

                                         Makes 2½ cups.

## Plantation Hot Sauce

½ cup honey
½ cup prepared mustard
½ cup cider vinegar
¼ cup Worcestershire sauce

1 tablespoon chopped parsley
2 teaspoons liquid hot pepper
   sauce
1 teaspoon salt

In a 1-quart saucepan, blend honey and mustard; stir in remaining
ingredients. Bring to a boil. Serve with smoked fish or shrimp.

                                     Makes approximately 1½ cups.

## Cucumber Sauce I

1 tablespoon instant minced
   onion
1 tablespoon water
1 cup mayonnaise
2 tablespoons cucumber, peeled
   and chopped
1 tablespoon pitted green olives,
   chopped

1 tablespoon capers, drained and
   chopped
1 tablespoon parsley flakes
1 hard-cooked egg, chopped
2 teaspoons Worcestershire sauce
1 teaspoon prepared mustard
$1/16$ teaspoon garlic powder

Mix minced onion with water; let stand 10 minutes to rehydrate.
Combine rehydrated onion with remaining ingredients; mix well.
Serve with fried fish cakes.

Makes 1⅓ cups.

## Cucumber Sauce II

⅓ cup grated cucumber
1 teaspoon grated onion
¼ cup mayonnaise or salad
   dressing
2 teaspoons vinegar

½ cup dairy sour cream
2 teaspoons minced parsley
Salt to taste
$1/16$ teaspoon pepper

Grate the cucumber and onion; press in strainer to remove juice.
Add mayonnaise, vinegar, sour cream, parsley, salt, and pepper.

Makes 1 cup.

## Cucumber Dressing I

1⅓ cups peeled diced cucumber
1½ cups dairy sour cream
2 teaspoons salt

1 teaspoon sugar
2 tablespoons vinegar
1 teaspoon Angostura bitters

Chill and serve with cold rock lobster.

Makes 3 cups.

## Cucumber Dressing II

1 medium cucumber
¼ teaspoon salt

½ cup whipping cream
2 tablespoons vinegar

Peel cucumber, chop finely, and season with salt. Allow to drain thoroughly. Whip cream until thick but not stiff. Add vinegar gradually and continue beating until mixture is stiff. Fold in drained cucumber.

Makes 1 cup.

## Tangy Fish Sauce

¼ cup chopped celery
1 small clove garlic, minced
⅛ teaspoon dry mustard
2 tablespoons butter or margarine

1 can (11 ounces) Cheddar cheese
    soup
⅓ cup milk
1 tablespoon chopped dill pickle

In saucepan, cook celery with garlic and mustard in butter until tender. Add remaining ingredients. Heat; stir occasionally. Serve over cooked white fish.

Makes 1½ cups.

## Hawaiian Seafood Marinade

½ cup cider vinegar
⅔ cup oil
2 teaspoons salt
½ teaspoon white pepper

½ cup minced onion
1½ cups unsweetened pineapple
    juice

Blend all ingredients together. Pour over frozen butterflied lobster tails (rock or Icelandic lobster, prawn, or shrimp) which are meat-side down in shallow pan. Let tails stand until defrosted. Use as basting sauce during grilling.

Makes 2½ cups.

## Sweet 'n' Sour Sauce

¾ cup tarragon vinegar
¾ cup brown sugar
¾ cup water
1½ tablespoons soy sauce
½ teaspoon salt
2 tablespoons cornstarch

½ cup green pepper strips
¼ cup chopped green onions and
   tops
2 medium tomatoes, cut into
   sixths

Combine vinegar, sugar, ½ cup water, soy sauce, and salt. Bring to a boil and remove from heat. Combine ¼ cup water with cornstarch. Gradually add cornstarch paste to hot liquid, stirring constantly. Return to heat. Cook over moderate heat, stirring constantly, until mixture is thick and clear. Add green pepper and onion. Cook for 3 minutes. Add tomatoes. Serve over fried fish.

Makes 3½ cups.

## Tartar Sauce

1 cup mayonnaise or salad
   dressing
2 tablespoons chopped parsley
2 tablespoons finely chopped sweet
   pickle or drained pickle relish
2 tablespoons finely chopped pimiento-stuffed green olives

2 tablespoons finely chopped onion
1 teaspoon cream style prepared
   horseradish
1 teaspoon lemon juice
⅛ teaspoon Worcestershire sauce
⅛ teaspoon salt
Dash liquid hot pepper sauce

Combine all ingredients and mix well.

Makes 1½ cups.

## Béarnaise Sauce

*Béarnaise is a classic French sauce that originially was developed in the French province of Béarn. It is considered to be a superior sauce for fish.*

1 tablespoon chopped green onion
2 teaspoons lemon juice
¼ cup dry white wine
½ teaspoon dried tarragon leaves

¼ teaspoon dried chervil leaves
3 egg yolks
⅛ teaspoon cayenne pepper
½ cup margarine or butter

In small saucepan combine green onion, lemon juice, white wine, tarragon, and chervil. Simmer until mixture is reduced to about 2 tablespoons. Cool. Place egg yolks, cayenne, and herb mixture in blender container. Cover; quickly turn blender on and off. Heat margarine until melted and almost boiling. Turn blender on high speed; slowly pour in margarine, blending until thick and fluffy, about 30 seconds. Heat over warm, not hot, water until ready to serve.

Makes 1 cup.

## Horseradish Sauce

½ cup prepared horseradish
1 tablespoon all-purpose flour
¼ teaspoon paprika

½ teaspoon salt
1 cup half and half

In a small saucepan combine horseradish, flour, paprika, and salt. Stir in half and half. Cook until thickened, stirring constantly.

Makes 1½ cups.

## Cranberry Tartar Sauce

1 cup mayonnaise or salad
    dressing
½ cup jellied cranberry sauce
¼ cup undrained sweet pickle
    relish

2 tablespoons chopped onion
2 tablespoons chopped ripe olives,
    optional
2 tablespoons chopped parsley

Combine all ingredients. Chill thoroughly. Serve very cold.

Makes 1½ cups.

## Spanish Sauce

3 tablespoons salad oil or
    shortening
1½ cups strained tomatoes
¼ cup chopped green pepper
1 garlic glove, chopped
¼ cup chopped or thinly sliced
    mushrooms

¼ cup chopped onion
1 teaspoon lemon juice
1½ teaspoons Worcestershire
    sauce
1½ teaspoons prepared mustard
1½ teaspoons salt
Few grains cayenne

Heat oil in skillet. Add remaining ingredients. Simmer 20 minutes;
serve hot.

Makes 6 to 8 servings.

## Mornay Sauce

½ cup butter or margarine
¼ cup all-purpose flour
2 cups milk
¼ cup grated Parmesan cheese

¼ cup finely cut Swiss cheese
2 egg yolks
Salt and pepper to taste

Melt ¼ cup butter in 1-quart saucepan. Slowly blend in flour.
Gradually stir in milk and cook, stirring constantly, over medium
heat until mixture comes to a boil and thickens. Reduce heat, add
Parmesan and Swiss cheese, and stir until cheese melts. Remove
from heat. When ready to serve, beat egg yolks slightly in small
bowl. Gradually add small amounts of the hot milk mixture to the
egg, stirring constantly, until bowl feels warm to the touch. Then
slowly stir egg mixture into the milk mixture. Cut ¼ cup butter into
small pieces and stir into sauce. Add salt and pepper to taste. DO
NOT reheat sauce after adding the egg yolks or it will curdle.

Makes about 2½ cups.

## Amandine Sauce

¼ cup slivered blanched almonds
¼ cup butter or margarine

¼ teaspoon salt
1 teaspoon lemon juice

Carefully saute almonds in butter until golden brown. Season with salt; add lemon juice; serve warm.

Makes ½ cup or 4 servings.

## Spiced Tomato Sauce

2 cups tomatoes
2 sprigs parsley
¼ cup onion
1 teaspoon salt
2 whole peppercorns

2 whole cloves
1 whole allspice
3 tablespoons fat
3 tablespoons all-purpose flour

Simmer tomatoes, parsley, onions, and seasonings for 10 minutes. Remove whole spices. Melt fat; in a saucepan; blend in flour and gradually add the tomato mixture. Cook until thick, stirring constantly. Use as a sauce in which to bake or poach fish or use separately as a sauce accompaniment to fish.

Makes 6 servings.

## Court Bouillon Sauce

1½ cups dry white wine
1½ cups cold water
½ medium onion, sliced
1 tablespoon parsley, chopped
1 teaspoon salt

½ teaspoon thyme
1 cup white grapes
5 tablespoons butter
1½ tablespoons all-purpose flour
1 cup cream

Mix first 6 ingredients in a 2-quart saucepan. Bring just to a boil and simmer until mixture is reduced to one-half content, approximately 30 minutes. Strain through a fine strainer. Add grapes to mixture and let sit for 15 minutes. In a small saucepan, melt butter and thicken with flour. Add to bouillon mixture; stir until well blended. Add cream and cook over low heat for 3 to 5 minutes, stirring constantly.

Makes about 2½ cups.

## Cocktail Sauce

½ cup catsup
6 tablespoons lemon juice
1 tablespoon horseradish

3 drops liquid hot pepper sauce
½ teaspoon celery salt
¼ teaspoon salt

Blend all ingredients and chill.

Makes 6 servings.

## Mushroom-Walnut Sauce

3 tablespoons margarine or butter
1 tablespoon minced onion
1 cup sliced mushrooms (about ¼
    pound)
3 tablespoons all-purpose flour

½ teaspoon dry mustard
½ teaspoon salt
¼ teaspoon thyme
2 cups half and half
¼ cup toasted walnuts

In a saucepan melt 3 tablespoons margarine. Add onion and mush-rooms, and cook until tender. Stir in flour, mustard, salt, and thyme. Gradually stir in half and half. Cook over medium heat until thick-ened, stirring constantly. Stir in nuts. Serve sauce over fish and wild rice.

Makes 2½ cups.

## Smokey Fish Dip

¾ pound smoked mullet, mack-
    erel, or other smoked fish
1 package (8 ounces) cream cheese,
    softened

2 tablespoons lemon juice
½ teaspoon liquid smoke
¼ teaspoon garlic salt
2 tablespoons half and half

Remove skin and bones from fish. Flake the fish. Combine all ingredients and mix well. May be served with assorted crisp raw vegetables and/or crackers and chips.

Makes 2 cups.

## Worcester Clam Dip

1 cup dairy sour cream
1 can (7½ ounces) minced clams, drained
1 tablespoon chopped parsley

2 teaspoons onion powder
2 teaspoons Worcestershire sauce
¾ teaspoon lemon juice
⅛ teaspoon salt

In a small bowl combine all ingredients; mix well. Serve with carrot and celery sticks, potato chips, or crisp crackers.

Makes 1 cup.

## Arkansas Shrimp Dip

1 pound finely chopped cooked shrimp
1 package (8 ounces) cream cheese or Neufchatel cheese, softened
¼ cup dairy sour cream
1 tablespoon lemon juice

1 tablespoon minced onion
1 tablespoon minced green pepper
1 tablespoon minced celery
1 tablespoon minced green olives
4 drops liquid hot pepper sauce
Salt and pepper to taste

Combine shrimp, cheese, and sour cream. Add the remaining ingredients. Mix well and chill to blend flavors. Serve with crackers or fresh relishes.

Makes 2 cups.

## Smoked Salmon-Cheese Dip

1 cup flaked smoked salmon
½ pound very sharp cheese spread

Mayonnaise or salad dressing
Potato chips or crackers

Drain and flake salmon. Beat with rotary beater until salmon is light and fluffy. Add cheese and blend well. For sandwich spread, add mayonnaise until mixture has desired spreading consistency. For dip, more mayonnaise will be needed. Serve dip in a bowl surrounded with potato chips or crackers.

Makes 2 cups.

## Hot Crab Dip

½ pound regular crabmeat
1 package (8 ounces) cream cheese, softened
½ cup dairy sour cream
2 tablespoons mayonnaise or salad dressing
1 tablespoon lemon juice

1½ teaspoons Worcestershire sauce
½ tablespoon dry mustard
Pinch garlic salt
About 1 tablespoon milk
½ cup Cheddar cheese, grated
Paprika, for garnish

Remove cartilage from crabmeat. In large bowl, mix cream cheese, sour cream, mayonnaise, lemon juice, Worcestershire sauce, mustard, and garlic salt until smooth. Add enough milk to make mixture creamy. Stir in 2 tablespoons of the grated cheese. Fold crabmeat into cream cheese mixture. Pour into greased 1-quart casserole. Top with remaining cheese. Bake at 325 degrees F. until mixture is bubbly and browned on top, about 30 minutes. Serve with crackers.

Makes about 4 cups.

## Dilly Crab Dip

¾ pound blue crab clawmeat, fresh or pasteurized
1 egg
¾ cup salad oil
2 tablespoons lemon juice

1¼ teaspoons dry mustard
½ teaspoon dried dillweed
½ teaspoon salt
Dash white pepper

Remove any remaining pieces of shell or cartilage from crabmeat. Place egg, ¼ cup salad oil, lemon juice, dry mustard, dillweed, salt, and pepper in a blender container; cover. Blend for 5 seconds on high speed. Continue blending on high speed while adding remaining ½ cup salad oil in a slow steady stream. Turn blender off occasionally and clean sides of the container. Remove mixture from blender container to a 1-quart bowl. Stir in crabmeat. Chill at least 1 hour.

Makes 2½ cups.

## Crab Dip Margaret

1 pound crabmeat
1 cup dairy sour cream
½ cup mayonnaise

½ cup finely chopped onion
¼ cup sweet pickle relish
1½ tablespoons dark rum

Remove cartilage from crabmeat. Mix together sour cream, mayonnaise, onion, pickle relish, and rum. Add to crabmeat and mix thoroughly, but gently, with a fork. Chill thoroughly. Serve with crackers.

Makes about 4 cups.

## Great Lakes Dip

½ pound smoked whitefish or
   other smoked fish
1 cup dairy sour cream
2 tablespoons lemon juice
2 teaspoons chopped chives
1 teaspoon instant minced onion
½ teaspoon salt

¼ teaspoon dried rosemary
6 peppercorns, crushed
Dash ground cloves
Chopped parsley
Assorted chips, crackers, or raw
   vegetables

Remove skin and bones from the fish. Flake the fish. Combine all ingredients except parsley and crackers. Chill at least 1 hour to blend flavors. Sprinkle dip with parsley. Serve with chips, crackers, or vegetables.

Makes approximately 1¾ cups.

## Salmon Sandwich Spread

2 cups flaked salmon
1 cup chopped cabbage
⅓ cup grated carrot

1½ teaspoons catsup
⅓ cup mayonnaise
Salt to taste

Combine all ingredients except salt. Add salt to taste. Chill.

Makes 6 servings.

## Smoked Fish Spread I

1½ pounds smoked fish
1¼ cups mayonnaise or salad
    dressing
2 tablespoons finely chopped
    sweet pickle
2 tablespoons chopped parsley

1 tablespoon prepared mustard
2 teaspoons minced onion
2 teaspoons finely chopped celery
1 clove garlic, minced
Dash Worcestershire sauce

Remove skin and bones from fish. Flake the fish well. Combine all ingredients and mix well. Chill at least one hour.

Makes approximately 3½ cups.

## Smoked Fish Spread II

1½ pounds smoked fish
2 teaspoons minced onion
2 teaspoons finely chopped celery
1 clove garlic, minced
1¼ cups mayonnaise

2 tablespoons finely chopped
    sweet pickle
1 tablespoon prepared mustard
2 tablespoons chopped parsley
Dash Worcestershire sauce

Remove skin and bones from fish and flake well. Mix all ingredients together and chill one hour before serving. This recipe works especially well with smoked mullet.

Makes approximately 3½ cups.

## Shrimp Butter Spread

1 can (4½ ounces) shrimp
½ cup butter

1 tablespoon lemon juice

Drain shrimp. Combine in a mixing bowl with butter and lemon juice; work with a fork or sharp-edged pastry blender into a soft, spreading mixture. Refrigerate in a screw-cap jar. Soften at room temperature to spread.

*Flavor Foils*

a. Garlic discreetly. Crush one small clove around the bowl and remove before mixing . . . or add prepared garlic seasoning to taste.
b. Onion as you like it . . . 2 teaspoons, freshly grated, or other onion seasoning to taste.
c. Anchovy with restraint . . . 4 fillets, drained, worked into the basic mixture.
d. Cream cheese . . . for zest and for extending basic spread. Work in 3 ounces with a few drops liquid hot pepper sauce.

> Makes 1 cup or enough spread for about 90 party crackers or toast rounds.

# Shrimp Sandwich Filling

1 can (4½ ounces) shrimp
⅓ cup mayonnaise

2 teaspoons freshly grated onion or onion seasoning to taste, optional

Drain and chop shrimp. Combine with mayonnaise and onion.

*Variations on a Theme*

a. Add 2 hard-cooked eggs, sieved, and 1 tablespoon sweet pickle relish, drained.
b. Mix with ⅓ cup each chopped hearts of lettuce and crisp bacon crumbles.
c. Season with ½ teaspoon curry. Add 2 tablespoons raisins, ½ cup finely chopped celery.
d. Combine with 1 cup finely shredded cabbage and ½ cup finely chopped, unpeeled red apple.
e. Omit mayonnaise; blend with 3 ounces cream cheese and 3 tablespoons oil and vinegar dressing, 1 tablespoon chopped chives.

> Makes about 1 cup or filling for 6 sandwiches.

## Alaska King Crab Seafoam Salad Spread

½ cup Alaska king crab
⅛ cup roast beef
⅛ cup gherkins (dill)

1 cup whipped cream
2 teaspoons horseradish

Thaw crab and flake. Cut roast beef julienne. Mince gherkins. Blend horseradish with whipped cream. Combine all ingredients. Season to taste. Serve either as luncheon salad or as sandwich spread.

Makes 1 cup.

## Canapé and Sandwich Spread

1½ cups finely chopped cooked
    rock lobster meat
    (6 2-ounce tails)
⅓ cup celery, finely chopped
1½ tablespoons drained sweet
    pickle relish
6 stuffed olives, finely chopped

2 tablespoons chives
2 teaspoons lemon juice
2 hard-cooked eggs, finely
    chopped
1 teaspoon salt
Pepper to taste
½ cup mayonnaise

Mix all ingredients and chill.

Makes enough spread for 8
sandwiches or 24 canapés.

## Shrimp Canapé Paste

2 cups cooked shrimp
¼ cup catsup
¼ cup mayonnaise or salad
    dressing

2 tablespoons lemon juice
½ teaspoon salt
⅛ teaspoon dry mustard

Drain shrimp and grind fine. Combine remaining ingredients with shrimp; mix well. Use as canapé spread or with the addition of more mayonnaise for a dip.

Makes 2 cups.

## Salmon Avocado Spread

1 avocado, peeled, seeded, and grated
1 cup cooked salmon
1 tablespoon lemon juice
1 tablespoon mayonnaise or salad dressing

1½ teaspoons grated onion or 1 teaspoon onion salt
4 drops liquid hot pepper sauce
½ teaspoon salt
Paprika for garnish

Use a medium grater and grate the avocado into a bowl. Flake the salmon, remove skin if canned. Combine all ingredients. Mix lightly and pour into small bowl. Garnish with a little paprika and chill. Serve as a spread on various crackers or chips.

Makes 1½ cups.

## Tuna Sandwich Spread

1 can (9¼ ounces) tuna in vegetable oil
⅓ cup mayonnaise
1 teaspoon minced onion
¼ teaspoon salt

1 teaspoon lemon juice
1 teaspoon Worcestershire sauce
1 tablespoon capers, optional
¼ cup finely diced celery

Drain oil from tuna into mayonnaise; blend well. Add remaining ingredients to tuna. Stir with a fork until mixture is of fine consistency. Serve as a spread with rye or other breads.

Makes spread for 6 sandwiches.

# Halibut Sandwich Spread

2 cups poached flaked halibut
2 tablespoons lemon juice
2 teaspoons minced onion
½ cup finely chopped celery
3 tablespoons pickle relish
1 teaspoon Worcestershire sauce

½ teaspoon salt
4 dashes liquid hot pepper sauce
1 teaspoon prepared mustard
Mayonnaise or salad dressing to
moisten

Combine above ingredients. Use as a sandwich filling or as a spread for crackers or canapés.

Makes 3 cups.

# Squid Spread

3 pounds whole squid, fresh or
frozen
½ cup dairy sour cream
3 jars (2 ounces each) chopped
pimientos

½ cup mayonnaise
1 tablespoon lemon juice
1 teaspoon dried dillweed
Salt to taste

Thaw frozen squid. Clean squid if necessary. Cook mantles in boiling, salted water 1 hour or until tender; drain. Chop squid into small pieces; mix squid, sour cream, pimientos, and mayonnaise. Add lemon juice, dillweed, and salt. Serve chilled with crackers or assorted vegetables.

Makes approximately 6 cups.

# Cheese Stuffing

½ cup sliced onion
¼ cup butter or margarine
¾ teaspoon salt
Dash pepper

2 tablespoons chopped parsley
2 cups dry bread crumbs
1 cup grated Cheddar or Parmesan
cheese

Saute onion in butter until tender. Add to remaining ingredients and mix thoroughly.

For a 3- to 5-pound fish.

## Bread Stuffing

¾ cup chopped celery
3 tablespoons chopped onion
6 tablespoons melted butter
1 teaspoon salt

¼ teaspoon pepper
1 teaspoon thyme, sage, or dill
4 cups dry bread crumbs

Cook celery and onion in butter until tender (about 10 minutes). Add to bread crumbs. Blend in seasonings and mix thoroughly. If very dry, add 2 tablespoons water, milk, or fish stock.

For a 3- to 5-pound fish.

## Mushroom Stuffing

¼ cup minced celery
¼ cup minced onion
¼ cup butter or margarine
¼ to ½ pound sliced fresh
   mushrooms

1 tablespoon minced parsley
2 cups coarsely crushed crackers
¼ teaspoon poultry seasoning
½ teaspoon salt

In a large skillet saute the minced onion and celery in butter until golden; add the mushrooms, cook 3 minutes. Add parsley and the rest of the ingredients.

For a 4- to 6-pound fish.

## Raisin Stuffing

3 cups soft bread crumbs
3 tablespoons butter
2 cups boiling water
½ cup seedless raisins
½ cup chopped walnuts or pecans

1 egg, beaten
1 teaspoon salt
⅛ teaspoon pepper
½ teaspoon marjoram

Pour melted butter over crumbs and mix lightly. Pour boiling water over raisins and allow to stand for 5 minutes. Drain raisins and mix with nuts, beaten egg, salt, pepper, and marjoram. Mix with bread crumbs.

For a 3- to 4-pound fish.

## Whole Wheat Surprise Stuffing

1 cup chopped celery
1 cup chopped celery leaves
2 small onions, finely chopped
¼ cup butter or margarine
½ pound sliced mushrooms
1 loaf whole wheat bread,
     crumbed

2 teaspoons poultry seasoning
1 teaspoon salt
⅛ teaspoon pepper
1 bottle (8 ounces) stuffed olives,
     chopped

Saute celery, leaves, and onion in butter until onion becomes translucent. Add mushrooms and cook 5 minutes longer. Combine with crumbs; add seasonings and olives. Place stuffing on one side of fillet; place other fillet on top and sew fish together. Lay fish on greased baking sheet and bake at 425 degrees F., allowing 10 minutes per pound. Baste frequently—the fish should be tender but not dry. Serve with a rich white sauce combined with hard-cooked egg slices.

For a 3- to 5-pound fish.

## Oyster or Clam Stuffing

½ cup chopped oysters or clams
2 cups fine cracker crumbs
2 tablespoons melted butter
1 teaspoon salt

2 teaspoons chopped sweet or dill
     pickle, as preferred
2 tablespoons lemon juice
½ cup water

Mix ingredients in order given. If dressing seems dry, add more water. If desired, oyster or clam liquor may be substituted for part of the water.

For a 3- to 4-pound fish.

# Sweet Pickle Stuffing for Baked Fish

2 cups bread crumbs
¼ cup chopped sweet pickle relish
1 tablespoon lemon juice
1 tablespoon minced onion
½ teaspoon salt

¼ teaspoon pepper
1 teaspoon chopped parsley
3 tablespoons melted shortening
    or drippings

Combine all the ingredients. Stuff the cavity loosely with the mixture before baking.

For a 3- to 5-pound fish.

# Index

## A

Alaskan King Crab(s)
  Alaskan Appetizer Pie, 24
  Alaskan King Crab Seafoam
    Salad Spread, 170
  King Kabob Salad, 44
  Sitka Regal Rarebit, 126
Amondine Sauce, 162-63
Anchovy Sauce, 156
Antipasto Salad, 41
Arkansas Shrimp Dip, 165
Atlantic City Flamed
  Sea Bass, 76-77

## B

Baked Sea Bass, St. Helena, 72
Baked Stuffed Scallops, 134-35
Bake Sole Gourmet, 63
Batter Fried Shrimp, 113
Béarnaise Sauce, 160-161
Biscuit Topping, 127
Black Drum with Zesty Sauce, 108
Blender Hollandaise Sauce, 152
Blueberry Sauce, 63
Blue Crab(s)
  Country Crab Soup, 27
  Crab, Shrimp, and Okra
    Gumbo, 121
  Crab Chops, 122
  Crabmeat Cakes, 123
  Dilly Crab Dip, 166
  Maryland Deviled Crab, 124
Bluefish
  Delmarvelous Bluefish, 70
  Oven-Fried Bluefish, 66-67
Boiled Dungeness Crab, 124-25
Boiled Lobster, 112-13
Boston Bean Skillet, 99
Bread Stuffing, 173
Broiled Salmon Steaks with Currant-Lemon Barbecue Sauce, 55
Broiled Sesame Mullet, 81
Butterfish in Spanish Sauce, 98-99

## C

Calamary Mediterranée with
  Caper Sauce, 27
Canapé and Sandwich Spread, 170
Cape Cod Turkey with
  Egg Sauce, 58-59
Caper Sauce, 27
Carolina Shrimp Pilau, 118
Caviar Soufflé, 104
Ceviche, 67
Cheese Pastry, 92
Cheese Sauce, 153
Cheese Stuffing, 173
Clam(s)
  Clam Fritters, 132-33
  Clam Potato Salad, 50
  Clam Stuffing, 174
  Family Clam Bake, 132
  New England Clam Chowder,
    31
  Pilgrims Clam Pie, 130
  Puget Sound Clams in Shells,
    129
  Razor Clam Aspic, 50
  Razor Clam Crumb Pie, 131
  Worcester Clam Dip, 165
Cocktail Sauce, 35, 164
Cod
  About Dried Salt Codfish, 58
  Cape Cod Turkey with Egg
    Sauce, 58-59
  Codfish Balls, 58
  Cod Stuffed Potatoes, 60
  Hawaiian Kabobs Teriyaki, 56
Cool Blender Sauce, 156
Connecticut Planked Shad, 104
Cornish Crab, 122-23
Country Crab Soup, 27
Court Bouillon Sauce, 163
Crab(s). *See also* Alaskan King
  Crab(s), Blue Crab(s), Dungeness
  Crab(s).
  Alaskan Appetizer Pie, 25

Cornish Crab, 122-23
Country Crab Soup, 27
Crab, Shrimp, and Okra
  Gumbo, 121
Crab Dip Margaret, 167
Crab Louis, 46
Creole Bouillabsisse, 32
Hot Crab Dip, 166
Kodiak Crab Sandwiches,
  24-25
Maryland Deviled Crab, 124
Quick Seafood Casserole, 126
Seafood Cocktail, 23
Seafood Tomato Aspic, 51
Crab, Shrimp, and Okra Gumbo,
  121
Crab Chops, 122
Crab Dip Margaret, 167
Crab Louis, 46
Crabmeat Cakes, 123
Cranberry Sauce, 57
Cranberry Tartar Sauce, 161
Crawfish
  Crawfish Bisque, 28-29
  Crawfish Canapé
    "Jacob Astor", 21
  Crawfish "Skandia", 135
  Écrevisse Polynaise, 137
  Mousse of Crawfish, 136
  Pâté Chaud of Crawfish
    Forrestière, 136-37
Cream of Shrimp and Lettuce
  Soup, 30
Creamy Salmon Mold, 42
Creole Bouillabaisse, 32
Creole Jambalaya, 111
Croaker
  Lemon Garlic Croaker, 71
Croquettes, Seafood, 83
Cucumber Dressing I, 158
Cucumber Dressing II, 158
Cucumber Sauce, 90
Cucumber Sauce I, 158
Cucumber Sauce II, 158
Curried Shrimp and Potato Puff
  Casserole, 145

D
Delmarvelous Bluefish, 70
Deluxe Baked Scallops, 134
Diamond Jim Flounder, 64-65

Dill Sauce, 156
Dilly Crab Dip, 166
Door County Fish Boil, 98
Dover Sole Sunriver, 69
Drawn Butter, 161
Drawn Butter Sauce, 151
Dressings
  Whipped Cream Dressing, 51
Drum, Black
  Black Drum with Zesty
    Sauce, 108
Drum, Red
  Creole Bouillabaisse, 32
  Gulf Court Bouillon, 85
Dungeness Crab(s)
  Boiled Dungeness Crab, 124-25
  Crab Louis, 46

E
Easy Tomato Sauce, 153
Easy Tuna Coleslaw, 47
Écrevisse Polynaise, 137
Egg Sauce, 152, 153

F
Family Clam Bake, 132
Fillet of Sole Florentine, 70
Fillet of Sole Veronique, 68-69
Fish Cakes, Smorgasbord, 84
Fisherman Potatoes au Gratin, 105
Fish Muddle, 66
Fish Steaks Baked-in-the-Coals,
  107
Florida Red Snapper, 72-73
Florida Stone Crab Claws à la
  Kennedy, 125
Flounder
  Diamond Jim Flounder, 64-65
  New Bedford Flounder
    Roll-ups, 61
  New Bedford Walnut Fried
    Flounder, 61
Fluffy Lemon Sauce, 155

G
Garden Style Squid, 140
Golden Brown Sardine Appetizers,
  24
Golden Fried Shrimp, 117
Golden Halibut Bits, 81

Great Lakes Dip, 167
Green Goddess Shrimp Salad, 44-45
Grouper
    Plantation Fish in Aspic, 49
    Super Grouper, 87
Gulf Court Bouillon, 85

## H
Haddock
    Fish Muddle, 66
    Philadelphia Harborside Hash, 59
    Sandy Bog Fillets, 57
Halibut
    Golden Halibut Bits, 81
    Halibut Corn Chowder, 82-83
    Halibut Pot Roast, 83
    Halibut Sandwich Spread, 172
Hawaiian Kabobs Teriyaki, 56
Hawaiian Seafood Marinade, 159
Heritage Scalloped Oysters, 129
Hollandaise Sauce, 152; Blender
    Hollandaise Sauce, 152
Horseradish Sauce, 161
Hot Crab Dip, 166

## J
Jambalaya, 146
Jiffy Shrimp Jambalaya, 114-15

## K
King Kabob Salad, 44
King Mackerel
    King Mackerel Steaks with
        Sauce Provençale, 74-75
    Marinated King Mackerel,
        Norfolk Style, 75
    Smokey Fish Dip, 164

## L
Lemon Garlic Croaker, 71
Lemon Garlic Sauce, 154
Lemon Mustard Sauce, 155
Lemon Sauce I, 154
Lemon Sauce II, 154
Lingcod
    Sourdough Fried Fish with
        Blueberry Sauce, 62-63

Lobster
    Boiled Lobster, 112-13
    Canapé and Sandwich Spread, 170
    Lobster House Special, 112
    Lobster Salad, 45

## M
Marguery Sauce, 65
Marinated King Mackerel, Norfolk
    Style, 75
Maryland Deviled Crab, 124-25
Molded Salmon Salad, 41
Mornay Sauce, 162
Mousse of Crawfish, 136
Mullet
    Broiled Sesame Mullet, 81
    Mullet Macaroni Salad, 42
    Mullet Mobile, 82
    Plain Delicious Smoked Fish, 26
    Smoked Fish Cakes, 80
    Smokey Fish Dip, 164
    Smokey Mullet Dinner Salad, 43
    Smokey Seafood Salad, 48
    Tantalizing Mullet Salad, 43
Mustard Sauce, 71, 155

## N
New Bedford Flounder Roll-Ups, 61
New Bedford Walnut Fried
    Flounder, 61
New England Clam Chowder, 31

## O
Ocean Perch
    Boston Bean Skillet, 99
Octopus. See Squid.
Outer Banks Stuffed Spanish
    Mackerel, 76
Oven-fried Bluefish, 66-67
Oyster(s)
    Creole Bouillabaisse, 32
    Heritage Scalloped Oysters, 129
    Oyster Loaf, 128
    Oyster or Clam Stuffing, 175
    Oyster Pie Rappahannock, 127
    Oysters Rockefeller, 127

## P

Parsley Sauce, 153
Pastry, Cheese, 92
Pâté Chaud of Crawfish Forrestière, 136-37
Penobscot Bay Fish Pudding, 105
Perch
        Perch Turbans à la Newburg, 86-87
Petrale in the Classic Manner, 68
Philadelphia Harborside Hash, 59
Pickled Herring—Norwegian Style, 23
Pickled Rock Shrimp, 36-37
Pickled Salmon, 24
Pickled Shrimp, 116-17
Pie(s)
        Alaskan Appetizer Pie, 25
        Cheese Pastry, 92
        Oyster Pie Rappahannock, 127
        Pilgrims Clam Pie, 130
        Quick Deep Dish Salmon Pie, 90-91
        Razor Clam Crumb Pie, 131
        Salmon-Cheese Pie, 91
        Salmon Pie—Russian Style, 97
        Salmon Supper Pie, 92
        Squid Pie, 140
Pike. See Walleyed Pike.
Pilgrims Clam Pie, 130
Pimiento Cheese Sauce, 157
Plain Delicious Smoked Fish, 26
Planked Maine Sardines, 107
Plantation Fish in Aspic, 48-49
Plantation Hot Sauce, 157
Pollock
        Pollock Barbecue, 89
        Special Day Pollock, 88
Polynesian Rock Shrimp Salad, 47
Pompano en Papillote, 106-7
Pork Sauce, 60-61
Portuguese Fisherman Stew, 77
Potlatch Salmon, 97
Puget Sound Clams in Shells, 129

## Q

Quick Deep Dish Salmon Pie, 90-91
Quick Salmon Rice Casserole, 93

## R

Raisin Stuffing, 173
Razor Clam(s). See also Clam(s).
        Razor Clam Aspic, 50
        Razor Clam Crumb Pie, 131
Red Snapper
        Florida Red Snapper, 72-73
        Red Snapper with Vegetable Sauce, 73
Rémoulade Sauce, 33
Rockfish. See Striped Bass.
Rock Shrimp. See also Shrimp.
        Pickled Rock Shrimp, 36-37
        Polynesian Rock Shrimp Salad, 47
Roquefort Sauce, 157

## S

Salmon
        Broiled Salmon Steaks with Currant-Lemon Barbecue Sauce, 55
        Creamy Salmon Mold, 42
        Molded Salmon Salad, 41
        Pickled Salmon, 24
        Potlatch Salmon, 95
        Quick Deep Dish Salmon Pie, 90-91
        Quick Salmon Rice Casserole, 93
        Salmon Avocado Spread, 171
        Salmon Casserole Surprise, 97
        Salmon-Cheese Pie, 91
        Salmon in Cheese, 94
        Salmon Loaf, 90
        Salmon Pie—Russian Style, 97
        Salmon Piquante, 95
        Salmon Pudding—Norwegian Style, 96-97
        Salmon Romanoff, St. George, 94
        Salmon Sandwich Spread, 167
        Salmon Scandia, 93
        Salmon Supper Pie, 92
        Smoked Salmon-Cheese Dip, 165
        Twice-Canned Salmon, 96
Salmoncado Buns, 89
Sanddabs, Grant Avenue, 100

Sauces
    Amondine Sauce, 162-163
    Anchovy Sauce, 156
    Béarnaise Sauce, 160-61
    Blender Hollandaise Sauce,
        108
    Blueberry Sauce, 63
    Cocktail Sauce, 35, 164
    Cool Blender Sauce, 156
    Court Bouillon Sauce, 163
    Cranberry Sauce, 57
    Cranberry Tartar Sauce, 161
    Cucumber Sauce, 90, 158
    Dill Sauce, 156
    Drawn Butter Sauce, 151
    Egg Sauce, 152, 153
    Fluffy Lemon Sauce, 155
    Hollandaise Sauce, 152
    Horseradish Sauce, 161
    Lemon Garlic Sauce, 154
    Lemon Mustard Sauce, 155
    Lemon Sauce I, 154
    Lemon Sauce II, 154
    Marguery Sauce, 162
    Mornay Sauce, 162
    Mustard Sauce, 71, 155
    Newburg Sauce, 88
    Parsley Sauce, 153
    Plantation Hot Sauce, 157
    Pork Sauce, 61-62
    Rémoulade Sauce, 33
    Roquefort Sauce, 157
    Sauce à la Kennedy, 125
    Sauce Provençale, 75
    Seafood Cocktail Sauce, 35
    Smorgasbord Sauce, 84-85
    Sour Sauce for Special Day
        Pollock, 88
    Svenskie Sauce, 102-3
    Vegetable Sauce, 91
Seafood Cocktail, 23
Seafood Cocktail Sauce, 35
Seafood Croquettes, 83
Seafood Gumbo, 144
Seafood Tomato Aspic, 51
Sea 'n' Ranch Salad, 46-47
Sea Scallops—in Shells, 133
Sea Trout
    Creole Bouillabaisse, 32
Shad Roe
    Soufflé, 104

Sheepshead with Drawn Butter,
    100-1
Shrimp
    Arkansas Shrimp Dip, 165
    Crab, Shrimp, and Okra
        Gumbo, 121
    Cream of Shrimp and Lettuce
        Soup, 30
    Creole Bouillabaisse, 32
    Curried Shrimp and Potato
        Puff Casserole, 145
    Golden Fried Shrimp, 117
    Green Goddess Shrimp Salad,
        44-45
    Jambalaya, 146
    Pickled Rock Shrimp, 36-37
    Polynesian Rock Shrimp, 119
    Savannah Stuffed Shrimp, 119
    Seafood Cocktail, 23
    Seafood Gumbo, 144
    Shrimp à la King, 120
    Shrimp and Corn Pudding, 115
    Shrimp Boil, 35
    Shrimp Butter Spread, 168-69
    Shrimp Canapé Paste, 171
    Shrimp Christmas Tree, 34-35
    Shrimp Creole, 144-45
    Shrimp Étouffée, 120
    Shrimp 'n Shell Casserole,
        118-19
    Shrimp Paste Charleston, 22
    Shrimp Sandwich Filling, 169
    Shrimp Supreme, 117
    Shrimp Toast, 22-23
Sitka Regal Rarebit, 126
Smoked Fish
    Great Lakes Dip, 167
    Plain Delicious Smoked Fish,
        26
    Smoked Fish Cakes, 80
    Smoked Fish Spread I, 168
    Smoked Fish Spread II, 168
    Smoked Salmon-Cheese
        Dip, 165
    Smokey Fish Dip, 164
    Smokey Mullet Dinner Salad,
        43
    Smokey Seafood Salad, 48
Smorgasbord Sauce, 84-85
Snow Crab. See Alaskan King
    Crab(s) and Crab(s).

Sole
  Bake Sole Gourmet, 63
  Ceviche, 67
  Dover Sole Sunriver, 69
  Fillet of Sole Florentine, 70
  Fillet of Sole Veronique, 68-69
  Petrale in the Classic Manner,
    68
  Sole Fillets Thermidor, 65
  Turban of Sole, 146-47
Sourdough Fried Fish with
  Blueberry Sauce, 62-63
Soufflé (caviar or shad roe), 104
Spanish Mackerel
  Outer Banks Stuffed Spanish
    Mackerel, 76
  Plain Delicious Smoked Fish,
    26
  Smokey Fish Dip, 164
  Texas Grilled Spanish
    Mackerel, 74
Special Day Pollock, 88-89
Spicy Sauce, 153
Squid
  Calamary Mediterranée with
    Caper Sauce, 27
  Cleaning Octopus and Squid,
    139
  Garden Style Squid, 138-39
  Squid Fritters Americana,
    138-39
  Squid Pie, 140
  Squid Spread, 172
  Stuffed Squid Monterey, 139
Steamed Clams in Wine Broth, 36
Striped Bass
  Portuguese Fisherman Stew,
    77
Stuffed Squid Monterey, 139
Stuffing, Vegetable, 76
Super Grouper, 87
Svenskie Sauce, 102-3
Svenskie Smelt Fry, 102-3
Sweet 'n' Sour Sauce, 160

Sweet Pickle Stuffing for Baked
  Fish, 175

T
Tangy Fish Sauce
Tantalizing Mullet Salad, 43
Tartar Sauce, 160
Texas Grilled Spanish Mackerel, 74
Tomato Sauce, 153; Easy Tomato
  Sauce, 153
Tuna
  Antipasto Salad, 41
  Easy Tuna Coleslaw, 47
  San Pedro Tuna Omelet, 78
  Sea 'n' Ranch Salad, 46-47
  Tuna and Corn Casserole, 79
  Tuna and Noodles Italian
    Style, 80
  Tuna Salad Filled Tomatoes,
    48
  Tuna Sandwich Spread, 171
Turban of Sole, 146-47
Twice-Canned Salmon, 96

V
Vegetable Sauce, 91
Vegetable Stuffing, 76
Vinegar Sauce, 151

W
Walleyed Pike
  Winnibigoshish Walleye and
    Wild Rice, 103
Whipped Cream Dressing, 51
Whitefish
  Door County Fish Boil, 98
  Great Lakes Dip, 167
White Sauce, 153
Whiting, Gloucester Style, 101
Whole Wheat Surprise Stuffing, 174
Winnibigoshish Walleye and Wild
  Rice, 103
Worcester Clam Dip, 165